ConAgra Foods®

It was easy to say "yes" when Burt Wolf invited ConAgra Foods® to help bring his *What We Eat* series to national public television.

Coming from an internationally syndicated television journalist with a special interest in the history of American food, Burt's invitation was indeed an honor.

ConAgra Foods shares Burt's passion for food and his fascination with the ever-changing American appetite.

By understanding the way America eats and quickly responding with the wholesome new products America wants, ConAgra Foods' brands like Healthy Choice®, Reddi-wip®, Butterball®, and many more have earned their place in 99 percent of all U.S. kitchens.

Thank you for inviting ConAgra Foods into your homes and into your lives.

We are very proud to set America's table.

Bruce Rohde
Chairman and Chief Executive Officer
ConAgra Foods, Inc.

What We Eat

THE TRUE STORY OF WHY WE PUT SUGAR IN OUR COFFEE AND KETCHUP ON OUR FRIES

EDITED BY BURT WOLF

TEHABI BOOKS

TEHABI BOOKS

Tehabi Books developed, designed, and produced the companion book to the series *What We Eat* and has conceived and produced many award-winning books that are recognized for their strong literary and visual content. Tehabi works with national and international publishers, corporations, institutions, and nonprofit groups to identify, develop, and implement comprehensive publishing programs. Tehabi Books is located in San Diego, California. www.tehabi.com

President and Publisher Chris Capen
Senior Vice President Tom Lewis
Vice President of Operations Sam Lewis
Editorial Director Nancy Cash
Sales Director Eric Pinkham
Director, Trade Relations Marty Remmell
Senior Art Director Josie Delker
Production Artist Kendra Triftshauser
Editor Sarah Morgans
Copy Editor Jacqueline Garrett

For more information on corporate custom publishing, contact Eric Pinkham, Sales Director, at Tehabi Books, 4920 Carroll Canyon Road, Suite 200, San Diego, California 92121-3735; or, by telephone, at 800-243-7259.

Please see page 176 for photo credits.

Library of Congress Cataloging-in-Publication Data is on file.
ISBN 1-887656-98-7

First Edition

Printed through Dai Nippon Printing Co., Ltd. in Korea

10 9 8 7 6 5 4 3 2 1

The paper used in this publication meets the minimum requirements of the American National Standard for Information Sciences—Permanence of Paper for Printed Library Materials, ANSI Z39.48-1992.

Making One World Out of Two

Originally, every plant and animal that lived on land lived on one giant continent. About 180 million years ago, forces inside the earth began breaking that landmass into the continents we have today. It was a centrifugal force and it continued to push the continents and everything that lived on them farther and farther apart.

But slightly over five hundred years ago a counter force appeared and started pulling everything back together. Only this time it wasn't a geological force inside the earth, it was the force of human culture, and the point man was Christopher Columbus. During the ten years between Columbus' first voyage in 1492 and his fourth and final trip in 1502, new forces were set in motion that totally changed the course of history and continue to affect our daily lives.

Millions of people moved or were forced to move from one continent to another, governments changed their structures, religions were exported, and capitalism began to take hold. But surprisingly, some of the most important changes were not the result of politics or religion; they were the result of the plants and animals that were exchanged between two worlds.

We call them the Old World and the New World, but I think that what we really had were two old worlds. After all, it looks like people have been living in the Americas for 35,000 years and even to a man my age, that's a long time. What Columbus did was introduce the two worlds to each other—the result was one new world. And the exchange of plants and animals between the two old worlds changed what people ate and why, and that fundamental shift changed almost everything on our planet. The television series from which this book has been drawn looks at those changes and how they continue to influence our lives.

Burt Wolf
New York City
1 August 2002

THE STORY OF THE
Tomato

When the first Spanish explorers arrived in Mexico, it was under Aztec rule. The Aztecs had been in control of Mexico and Central America since 1325 A.D. and had solidified their power by conquering earlier indigenous cultures and dominating the trading markets. Between conquering and trading, the Aztecs came in contact with many different cultures, which exposed them to many new foods. The Maya probably introduced the Aztecs to the tomato, which they immediately accepted because it reminded them of something they were already eating—the *tomatillo*, or husk tomato. The Aztecs would juice them, add chili peppers, and grind in a bit of pumpkin seed, creating a salsa.

The Spanish eventually conquered the Aztecs. The first time the Spanish ran into the tomato was when Cortés marched into Mexico in 1519. The Spanish called it a *tomate*.

The Spanish sent tomatoes from Mexico to their settlements in the Caribbean and from there back to southern Europe, where the tomato flourished in the Mediterranean climate. The earliest published description of tomatoes in Europe appeared in Italy in 1544. They came to be called *pomi d'oro*, which means "golden apples." Tomatoes were associated with the yellow fruit of the mandrake plant, which was described in the Bible as an aphrodisiac. In many European countries the tomato became known as a "love apple."

The red, ripe orb we call the tomato is actually a fruit, not a vegetable. The well-loved role it plays in savory dishes transformed it in conventional wisdom into a vegetable, and a Supreme Court decision codified that transformation in the 1890s.

TURNING A FRUIT INTO A VEGETABLE

Although the tomato has been considered the "Queen of America's Vegetables," the tomato is a fruit, not a vegetable. The definition is very straightforward. Parts of edible plants that do not carry a seed used for reproduction are vegetables: carrots, celery, lettuce, beets— no seeds. The portions of a plant that carry a seed used for reproduction are fruits: apples, pears, grapes, and watermelons all come with seeds. The tomato has a seed for reproduction; therefore, the tomato is a fruit.

Before the Civil War, most commercially grown tomatoes were raised in the South and transported to northern cities. During the war that supply was cut off, so farmers in the Bahamas and other parts of the Caribbean started planting tomatoes and exporting them to the States. After the war, the Caribbean tomato trade expanded and began to threaten the profits of many U.S. growers. To protect American growers against this competition, Congress passed the Tariff Act of 1883. It levied a ten-percent duty on imported vegetables.

In the spring of 1886, John Nix imported a shipment of tomatoes from the Caribbean to New York, maintaining that they were a fruit rather than a vegetable. Nix paid the duty under protest and then brought suit to get his money back. After six years of winding through the courts, the case of *Nix v. Hedden* was argued before the Supreme Court. The Court decided that even though the tomato was botanically a fruit, it moved through commerce disguised as a vegetable and, being a vegetable, had to be protected. A ten-percent duty was its protection.

Tomatoes did well throughout southern Europe; the people of Spain, southern France, and Italy incorporated them—however slowly—into their diets. That changed during the seventeenth century when famine swept through Italy. Suddenly the tomato was valuable. Instructor of culinary history at the New School for Social Research in Manhattan Andrew F. Smith explains:

"When famines occurred, foods were needed quickly, and the tomato has the interesting characteristic that you put it in the ground and three months later you have a plant bearing fruit. And so the southern Italians very quickly found out that they liked the tomato, and in addition to that, it was a famine food that could be used in many different ways."

Tomatoes have always been a popular home garden crop because of their quick growing season and their prolific production.

KETCHUP: A COSMOPOLITAN CONDIMENT

The word *ketchup* comes with an image of a thick, sweet, tomato-based condiment that is poured, spooned, and squirted onto most of our foods. While bottles of tomato ketchup seem to grace the tables of every all-American restaurant, Americans did not create ketchup, and ketchup, in its origin, was not thick, sweet, or tomato-based.

Ketchup's earliest incarnation was as a fish sauce in China and contained soybeans, not tomatoes.

"The word *ketchup* is originally from the Chinese . . . *kê-tsiap,*" explains culinary historian Andrew F. Smith. "It originally meant a fermented fish sauce or soy sauce . . . that was spiced and initially fermented into a very thin, liquid sauce that was used mainly in cooking. It was not used as a condiment.

"It migrated from China into Southeast Asia, and into Indonesia. And the Indonesians fell in love with it, which by then was called *ca-chop.* And it is still available in all sorts of different variations in Indonesia today."

British explorers, traders, and sailors moving through Asia came into contact with ca-chop. And when they got home they attempted to recreate the recipe. Soybeans did not grow easily in Europe, so British cooks substituted other products like anchovies, mushrooms, kidney beans, and, later in the eighteenth century, walnuts.

British colonists brought their ketchup recipes to America.

"It's really not until about 1800 that Americans start fooling around with other products, just like the British did, and created a whole series of other ketchups: fruit ketchup, cherry ketchup, peach ketchup, and so forth," relates Smith. "Somebody found that tomatoes made good ketchup, too. Up until about the Civil War . . . you would have had walnut ketchup, a mushroom ketchup, and tomato ketchup. If you went into the best restaurants of America at that time, at the bottom of their menus, they proudly announced that they had all three of these ketchups available."

After the Civil War, the price of tomatoes dropped dramatically. A quart of tomato ketchup, which sold for $2.50 in 1870, was selling for ten cents by the turn of the century. The price of mushrooms and walnuts remained high, and by 1896, the *New York Tribune* had declared tomato ketchup America's national condiment.

But tomatoes were not eaten in northern Europe. The English had a particular dislike for them. They were different from the other fruits and vegetables that grew in Great Britain, and they did not match up with the diet recommended by most physicians.

For centuries doctors practiced humoral medicine. All foods were divided into two groups, hot and cold, which were used to balance the humors of the body. In general, the more water a food held, the cooler it was. Tomatoes were considered very cool. If you were having a hot time—feeling irascible or passionate—doctors prescribed cool foods to bring you into line. If you were too cool—feeling sluggish or depressed—then hot foods were given to warm you up.

"And for the humoral system of medicine, what you do not want to do is eat a cold food in a cold country," explains Smith. "And they identified England and northern Europe as cold countries, and so you wouldn't want to eat tomatoes there. But it was perfectly all right for an Englishman to go to Italy or to Spain and eat a tomato, because then he was in a hot country, and therefore the balance between the hot country and the cold product was one that was good."

When the English began to take their holidays along the Mediterranean coast where tomatoes were part of everyday menus, they brought a taste for the tomato back to England. By the middle of the 1700s the tomato, as an edible plant, was being cultivated in England. Within a few decades most other northern European countries had added the tomato to their ingredient list.

Although northern Europeans were slow to accept tomatoes into their diets, tomatoes played a prominent role in the cooking of Italy, home to Milan's Piazza del Duomo.

THE DRINKABLE TOMATO

During the summer of 1917, Louis Perrin was the French–American chef at a resort in French Lick Springs, Indiana. One day he started serving his guests tomato juice. It was just an experiment, but the Chicago businessmen who spent their vacations in French Lick Springs loved it and spread the word: Tomato juice was great stuff.

By the 1920s, tomato juice was being promoted as a health drink. Canned tomato drinks were getting more popular, but none of the products yielded juice with just the right color and flavor, and the tomato solids settled at the bottom of the can or glass—not what the public wanted.

In 1924, Ralph Kemp of Frankfort, Indiana, began looking for a way to break tomato pulp into minute particles that would float in the juice. His solution was to use a viscolizer—previously employed in the manufacture of ice cream. It required a great deal of adaptation and took four years of experiments before Kemp finally

French Lick brand tomato juice is named for the resort town in Indiana where tomato juice was first popularized.

canned tomato juice successfully. In 1928 he initiated the first national advertising campaign for tomato juice. It was an instant nationwide hit.

One reason tomato juice was so successful was that it arrived as Prohibition left. A cocktail made of tomato juice and vodka was probably introduced by Ferdinand "Pete" Petiot at Harry's Bar in Paris. During the 1930s, Petiot moved to New York and introduced his creation to America. Eventually, he added Worcestershire sauce and called it a Bloody Mary.

Ernest Hemingway claims that he personally introduced the Bloody Mary to the bars of Hong Kong. He and his pals spent their evenings going from bar to bar teaching the bartenders how to properly prepare and serve the Bloody Mary.

The Bloody Mary, a cocktail made from tomato juice, vodka, and Worcestershire sauce, remains one of the few alcoholic beverages considered acceptable to consume before the cocktail hour.

In America, the acceptance of the tomato was divided along the Mason-Dixon line. In the South, tomatoes were part of the daily diet. In New England, however, tomatoes were not very important. They did not grow well, the varieties took longer to mature, and they were unlike any food that New Englanders were eating.

But that changed in 1834 when Dr. John Cook Bennett declared that the tomato would cure just about everything from dyspepsia to cholera. His claims were published in newspapers and magazines throughout the country. Bennett took a bunch of theories that had been circulating in the medical community and created a popular craze around the tomato.

THE TOMATO PILL

At one point in the mid-nineteenth century, health expert Dr. John Cook Bennett met Dr. Alexander Miles, who was busy selling a patent medicine called the "American Hygiene Pill." Bennett suggested to Miles that he change the name of his pill to "Extract of Tomato."

Miles began advertising his "Extract of Tomato," and newspapers in virtually every part of the country came through with headline articles on miraculous tomato cures. In 1843, *The Boston Cultivator* reported:

"We knew an instance of a very severe case of dyspepsia, of ten years standing, cured by the use of the tomato. The patient had been unable to get any relief; he could eat no fresh meat, nor boiled vegetables. Reading an account of the virtues of the tomato, he raised some, and used them as

In the first part of the nineteenth century, the tomato gained renown for its purported curative properties, and apothecaries began stocking medicines that mentioned the fruit-turned-vegetable on their labels. Few of these medicines actually contained any tomato.

food in the fall, stewed, and made some in a jelly for winter use. He was cured."

A publicity wave surged through every region of the nation, and Americans from all walks of life were infected with tomato mania. Even those who did not believe in tomato miracles believed the tomato to be a wholesome and delicious food.

Around 1840, the medical profession decided to investigate the tomato pills and find out what was really in them. All of their research suggested that there was nothing related to the tomato in any of the pills or liquid medicines. Ironic headlines, such as "Tomato Pills Will Cure All Your Ills," began to appear in the press. Nevertheless, Americans had started to eat more tomatoes.

Following pages: There are several hundred varieties of tomatoes with names such as the Green Zebra, Mountain Gold, Tommy Toe, Jubilee, Italian Oxheart, and Mister Stripey.

Tomatoes became even more important in North American cuisine when thousands of southern Italians immigrated to the United States. They planted tomatoes in their gardens, ate them raw, cooked with them, and introduced them to their non-Italian neighbors. Many Italian immigrants worked in grocery stores and restaurants and continued to spread the tomato. But it had to be in a form that was acceptable to mainstream America—Italian-American cuisine was born. By 1905, the first pizza parlors were opening up in New York City and the tomato hit the top of the charts—and the grocers' shelves.

Today there are more than five thousand varieties. One reason is that the tomato is self-pollinating: it can reproduce on its own. And every once in a while it changes its genetic code. If the new code produces a good tomato, the farmer keeps it.

A JUICY SPORT

During the late 1940s, tomato throwing became an organized event in Bunol, a town twenty-five miles west of Valencia, Spain. The Tomatina Festival, held on the last Wednesday in August, has been officially sponsored by the city since 1979. During the festival, more than thirty thousand people pelt each other and the city with tomatoes.

Throwing tomatoes is an American tradition that dates back to the middle of the 1800s. It started in rural areas at the end of the season when tomato prices had dropped so low that the tomatoes were not worth picking. People just tossed them at each other for sport.

Eventually it moved into urban theaters where it became one of the responses available to the audience—the critical counterbalance to throwing flowers. In recent years, target acquisition has been expanded to include politicians and other public figures.

Italian immigrants brought their love of the tomato to the United States, creating an Italian-American cuisine that became popular in mainstream America—most notably on pizza, with its essential tomato-based sauce. Not just for cooking, the tomato has been thrown for sport in Spain and to register criticism in America since the mid-1800s.

HOW THE
Potato
CHANGED THE WORLD

On two occasions the potato changed the course of world history. The first time was when, in the challenging agricultural environment of the Andes, it fed the army of workers who built the Incan Empire and then allowed the Spanish colonists who conquered them to feed the workforce that extracted the mineral wealth of South America. The second time was when potatoes helped fuel the expanding population of northern Europe as a handful of European nations began to dominate most of the world—which they did for over two hundred years.

Even the potato's greatest failure in Europe—the Irish potato famine of the 1840s—did its part to change history. It sparked a massive exodus of Irish, many of whom headed west, where they went on to shape, both physically and politically, the quickly growing United States.

Experts believe that the potato was first cultivated in the Andes Mountains of South America some seven thousand years ago. The great centers of pre-Inca culture were high up, as high as 12,500 feet above sea level, where each night the temperature would drop below freezing. Edible crops were in short supply in this environment, and the potato was one of the few crops that could be grown at high altitudes. The Andean farmers came to rely heavily on the potato—and they found an ingenious method of preserving their staple crop.

The fleshy tuber known as the potato is the fourth most important food crop in the world today because of its high nutritional value: a single medium-sized potato contains nearly half the adult daily requirement of vitamin C and more protein and calcium than comparable vegetables and grains. It's no wonder the potato has taken root in world culinary history.

Raw potatoes do not keep well, but by exposing their potatoes to the night air and then squeezing the water from them, Andean farmers were able to produce freeze-dried potatoes, called *chuño*, and they were able to store them in sealed, underground warehouses. The nutritional value of the potato is so high that you can live on them almost exclusively for a considerable length of time. They provide nearly everything a person needs, except calcium and vitamins A and D. And freeze-dried potatoes can hold their nutritional value for many years—they are an excellent hedge against crop failure and famine.

The Incan government collected the freeze-dried potatoes as tribute, kept them in imperial warehouses, and distributed them to workers who were employed on official projects. The potatoes ensured a stable food supply and made it possible for the Inca to maintain a civilized society, to wage wars and conquer territory, and to build their network of roads and cities. The conquering Spanish adopted the Incan system, and used the freeze-dried potatoes to feed the thousands of laborers they used to mine the mineral wealth of the Andes.

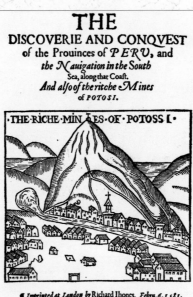

Silver was mined in Potosi Mountain in Bolivia.

In 1545, Spanish colonists discovered silver in Potosí Mountain in what is now southern Bolivia. Thousands of forced laborers were brought in to work the mines, and thousands of middlemen settled there, as one historian put it, to "mine the miners." By 1575, the mining town of Potosí was the largest—and richest—city in the Americas, with over 120,000 inhabitants, and it continued to grow as more fortune hunters arrived each day. An inexpensive food was needed to keep the workers alive—and freeze-dried potatoes did the job.

The silver taken out of the mines of South America flooded the rest of the world. In Europe, it allowed King Philip II and his successors to pay for Spain's imperial fleets and the armies that sailed with them. The windfall lasted for about a century; then the ore ran out, and Spain's political and military power began to decline.

The massive influx of silver from the Americas led to an unprecedented monetary inflation. Constantly rising prices upset the traditional social patterns and altered economic relations. Some people who where rich lost everything, and some people who were

In addition to developing bridges that helped them navigate the steep Andean mountains, dwellers of the Andes discovered that potatoes were one of the few crops that could be grown at high altitudes.

poor became fabulously rich. But in the end, it was not the silver that would prove most valuable to Europeans—it was the potato.

When the first Spanish ships arrived in the Western Hemisphere, they found that familiar staple foods like rice, wheat, barley, rye, and oats were entirely absent from the Americas. While Spanish settlers, who looked down on potatoes as fit only for Native American laborers, relied on corn as a substitute for European grains, the potato caught on among sailors, who may have recognized that the vitamin C–rich tubers were effective against scurvy. The first potatoes to reach Europe traveled on Spanish ships returning from South America. Leftover potatoes came ashore with the sailors, and a few of the men tried to grow them at home.

The dry Spanish plains did not welcome the potato, but the tuber did do well in the wet, high altitudes of the Pyrenees along the French border. By the end of the sixteenth century, potatoes were being grown by the Basques in northern Spain.

Even before Columbus's expeditions, Basque fishing fleets had been sailing across the North Atlantic and harvesting cod on the Grand Banks of Canada. As the cod fleets headed home from Canada, they would stop on the west coast of Ireland and dry their catch. Sometime in the late 1500s or early 1600s, some of those fishermen, who had become acquainted with potatoes at home, brought them to Ireland.

Spain also introduced it to the rest of Europe. During the 1500s, Spain was in control of parts of Italy, where farmers in the Po Valley just north of Milan began to adopt the potato. For most of the sixteenth century the Netherlands was also under Spanish rule. When the Dutch started fighting for their independence during the second half of the 1500s, they cut off Spain's northern shipping lanes, forcing the Spanish to reroute their supplies through the Mediterranean to Italy. From there, troops crossed the Alps on foot, making their way up through Alsace and into the Low Countries. This route connected Spain's imperial provinces and became known as the "Spanish Road." Potatoes took root in peasant gardens all along its path.

The potato originated in South America and spread to Europe with Spanish sailors. They were also brought to Spanish settlements, such as the sixteenth-century colony in Puerto Rico depicted above.

WARTIME SUSTENANCE

In the late sixteenth century, armies were expected to supply themselves with food from the countryside in which they were operating. Stores of grain in barns were easy pickings. As a result, wherever the local population depended on stored grain for their survival, starvation was the usual and expected result of major military campaigns.

One reason the potato became so popular was that the villagers who lived along the "Spanish Road" realized that potatoes could help them survive the brutal requisitioning that took place as the troops passed through. Although the soldiers of the sixteenth and seventeenth centuries loved pillaging, digging potatoes out of the ground was apparently beneath their dignity.

By the beginning of the 1700s, peasants in Prusia had learned that a potato crop could help keep them alive during times of war.

In 1758, the British set sail to seize the French-held Fortress of Louisbourg, Nova Scotia, in an effort to restore commerce to colonial New England.

The potato was the best—and cheapest—famine insurance they could find. During the 1740s, Fredrick the Great of Prussia realized the same thing and ordered his government to have potatoes planted throughout his kingdom. Free potato seeds were distributed with instructions on how the plant was to be cared for. As a result, even when French, Austrian, and Russian troops invaded Prussia during the Seven Years' War, Frederick's peasant farmers escaped disaster by eating potatoes. The potato helped ensure the survival of the Prussian state.

The armies that invaded Prussia became aware of benefits of the potato and brought the plant back to Austria, France, and Russia. In France, Antoine Augustin Parmentier, an army doctor who had lived on potatoes while serving time in a Prussian prisoner-of-war camp, became the potato's leading proponent.

Despite their suspicion of new foods, hard-pressed peasants in western France and southern Germany also came to value the potato. Farmers cultivated potatoes on a small but significant scale, primarily as a safeguard against marauding armies and failure of their grain crops. The potato eventually made its way from the family garden to the open fields. And as it entered the fields and kitchens of Europe, it once again changed the course of world history—but this time the process required some official intervention.

Around 1750, governments throughout Europe joined with landowners to press for the planting of potatoes. At the urging of a few dedicated botanists, they came to understand that, in spite of famine or war, potatoes could keep the peasants alive.

In contrast, a grassroots movement was responsible for the early expansion of the potato in Ireland. The landless workers who rented tiny plots from commercial farmers realized early on—as had the villagers along the Spanish Road—that unlike any other crop, the potato could sustain a poor family through times of hardship. And Irish peasants lived with terrible hardship.

In 1650, English military commander Oliver Cromwell, intent on subduing the rebellious Irish, resorted to a scorched earth policy.

Storehouses, mills, and fields were burned. Cromwell's troops even killed livestock in their determination to starve out rebel areas. It was in this setting that the value of the potato stood out. Potatoes grew underground, in small wet plots where they were difficult to burn. They stored safely and in concealed places within a farmer's cottage; they did not need to be milled or processed. Planting did not even require a plough—a family could plant an adequate crop using nothing more than a spade.

Following his campaign, Cromwell planned to replace the Catholic population of Ireland with Protestant veterans from his army. Irish landowners—who were Roman Catholics—were forced to exchange land owned in the East for poorer land in the West. The defeated Irish, who had grown a mixed crop of oats and potatoes, and supplemented their income and diets with cattle grazing, came to rely more and more heavily on the potato.

As the seventeenth century wore on, speculators—interested only in profit—bought out almost all of the land that had been occupied by Cromwell's veterans and their heirs. Raising cattle had long been the traditional safety net for Irish farmers, and many of these new landlords found that the best way to make money on Irish soil was commercial cattle grazing. They raised cattle, sent them to the

Shown at right, popular varieties of the potato include russets, round white, long white, round red, yellow flesh, and blue and purple varieties. Above: Oliver Cromwell.

ports of Dublin and Cork for slaughter, and shipped them abroad. By the beginning of the eighteenth century, Ireland had become Europe's leading exporter of beef.

At the same time, English commercial farmers were expanding their Irish operations, making Ireland an exporter of grains. But as commercial farming expanded, it left less and less arable land available for the native Irish. Under punitive English laws, Catholics were not allowed to buy land or hold onto a plot of land if Protestant land-lords could make a claim to it. They were forced to rent whatever leftover land they could find.

Commercial farmers and cattle graz-ers soon realized that English laborers lived on bread and cheese and were much more expen-

In 1842, economic conditions in Ireland led to Starvation Riots like the one depicted here at a Galway potato store.

sive to feed than the native Irish, who had learned to make do with a far cheaper diet of potatoes and milk. Though a potato diet may have been monotonous, along with milk to make up for the calcium and vitamins lacking in the potato itself, it was nutritionally ade-quate. Because even a small potato crop could produce so many calories, a single acre of pota-toes and a single cow could feed an entire Irish family. And given the shrinking amount of land available for rent, it was not uncommon for an Irish family to find itself with only a single acre.

The potato kept the poor of Ireland healthy, and the Catholic population increased rapidly over the course of the eighteenth century. The expanding population was highly suscepti-ble to shifts in the economy. A growing pool of laborers sought to supplement shrinking wages by raising a few pigs or by growing and selling exportable grain crops on plots of land, while they lived on potatoes.

The demand for land grew as the popula-tion increased, which drove up rents. And to make matters worse, English trade practices and a slackening of demand in Europe nearly destroyed the traditional Irish textile industry, leaving thousands unemployed. By the middle of the nineteenth century, the Irish—nearly eight million of them—were desperately poor, and becoming poorer.

During the first half of the nineteenth century tensions started rising: Irish Catholics began to demand their rights. English trade laws governing Ireland led to wild fluctuations in the prices of grain and other exports. That drove wages down even further. The Irish economy suffered under tariffs designed to protect English agriculture and industry. Ireland's poor, trapped by economic and political circumstances, were living more or less exclusively on potatoes.

But the terrible, unforeseen climax took place in 1845, when a sudden outbreak of blight—a particularly virulent fungus by the name of *Phytophthora infestans*, which had recently arrived from the United States—nearly destroyed the entire potato crop. The potato famine was disastrous.

The crop failed again in 1846 and in 1848. English tariffs prevented the emergency importation of substitute grains. Relief efforts eventually got underway, but they were too little, too late. In the end, in a three-year period, over a million people died of starvation and disease out of a population of only eight million. For many others, there was no choice but emigration.

THE IRISH COME TO AMERICA

By 1850 over a million people had left Ireland, with most immigrating to the United States. The Irish who arrived in the United States had an extraordinary impact on our history. Explains City University of New York history professor Edward T. O'Donnell, an expert on Irish-American history:

"The Irish, of course, have been coming since the colonial period. But their biggest wave was certainly in the nineteenth century, and one of their biggest contributions was arriving in such huge numbers. It forced America to rethink what it meant to be American, and expanded the definition. America was not particularly pleased with the arrival of the Irish, and it took a couple of generations to accept them as Americans.

"Probably the most evident contribution the Irish made is in the role that they played in building the American economy as laborers. They came with very few skills, with almost no money for the most part, but they did arrive with the need to work and the willingness to work. If you look across America, the great infrastructure that made America the greatest economy in the world by the early twentieth century—the railroads, the canals, the great projects like the Brooklyn Bridge—all were built overwhelmingly with Irish labor. Many other groups participated, too, but the Irish really were the key contributors to that development."

Potatoes had become a basic part of virtually every meal in the Irish peasant home. When the Irish refugees from the potato famine arrived in North America, they continued that tradition.

In the 1840s, over one million people died in Ireland when a fungus infected and destroyed the potato crops. The Irish Potato Famine led thousands of Irish to immigrate to the United States. The photograph on the following pages shows a few of those immigrants on Ellis Island in New York City, the gateway to a new life in America.

Despite the famine created in Ireland by the potato crop failure, overall the potato helped a few states in northern Europe build a political, industrial, and military base that gave them control over much of the planet. Although potato farming requires a bigger workforce than growing grain does, it yields two to four times as many calories per acre. As potatoes spread through Europe, a feedback process set in: more potatoes produced more calories, more calories produced a larger population, and a larger population produced more field workers, who produced more potatoes. More and more potatoes were planted and the population of northern Europe grew as fast as the potato plants. In fact, the rate of population growth in northern Europe far outstripped what was taking place in other parts of the world.

This potato patch near Dublin, Ireland, reveals the beauty that accompanies the potato plant.

While the European upper classes never gave up grain in favor of the potato, and grain remained dominant in agricultural commerce, the potato did become the staple food for the poor—and the new working classes across Europe. Nutrients from the potato contributed to a population increase that was big enough to supply not only the additional labor for field farming the potato, but the workforce Europe needed for its transformation into an industrial society.

Workers left the fields for the new factories that were made possible by the shift to fossil fuels like coal. Unlike the physical force needed by the Incas and Spaniards to drive workers into the mines, industrialists only needed to offer a subsistence wage for workers to come out of the countryside and into the mines and factories.

The rapidly growing European population also filled the ranks of the imperial armies and navies, and their victories throughout the world allowed millions of Europeans to migrate overseas.

The potato also helps explain the rise of northern Europe that started about 1750 and lasted for two hundred years. It is certain that without the extra food supplied by the potato, Germany and Russia would not have become leading industrial and military powers.

This lesson has not been lost on the developing world. Today, the potato is catching on in Africa and Asia, where nations struggling to feed hundreds of thousands of hungry people have been turning to the potato. In South Asia and in some parts of Africa, per capita potato consumption has outstripped consumption in many European countries. These days, Rwandans eat more potatoes than do the Irish.

FRIES AND CHIPS

Once the potato became a basic part of the peasant diet of Europe, it began its ascent to a higher social status. During the early 1800s, street vendors in Paris started offering slices of fried potato. They were shaped like a quarter moon and called *pommes de terre Pont-Neuf,* which translates as "New Bridge Potatoes." Named after of one of the bridges that cross the River Seine, they turned out to be an early form of the french fries eaten today. By 1870, fried potatoes had made their way across the channel to England, where street vendors put them together with fried fish to create England's national fast food. What Americans call french-fried potatoes are known as chips in England, and what Americans consider chips are called crisps in England. These days, Americans buy over three billion dollars' worth of potato chips each year. However, Americans eat most of their potatoes in the form of french fries. Each year, Americans consume over thirty pounds of french fries per person.

During the 1780s, Thomas Jefferson was our ambassador to France and seems to have spent much of his time in Paris drinking wine and collecting recipes. When he returned to the states he brought with him a recipe for perfect french-fried potatoes. A recipe for slices of deep fried potato shows up in an American cookbook dated 1878. But fries did not become very popular with Americans until the end of World War I, when American troops returned from the French front with a love of french fries.

They became even more popular during the 1930s when Americans started driving around the country in their own automobiles. Roadside restaurants began to serve fries because they were easily eaten in a car.

At the end of World War II there was a fantastic growth in the use of frozen foods, and the french-fried potato became a major item in the new frozen food cases that were being introduced in supermarkets. They also became the most popular food item in the restaurant business— for decades they have been the most profitable offering in fast food.

Today's most popular use of the potato is a deep-fried delicacy known as chips in England and french fries in the United States. The potato is a staple of the fast food industry.

THE STORY OF
CHILI PEPPERS

When Columbus set out from Spain, his objective was to get King Ferdinand and Queen Isabella into the black pepper business by establishing a route to the Indies across the Atlantic Ocean. At that time, the spice trade was dominated by Italian merchants who traded with the Arabs. The small, round, dry black pepper that we grind in a mill is native to India and was brought to ancient Greece and Rome by Arab traders. It was so valuable in fifteenth-century Europe that both the Spanish and the Portuguese spent fortunes sending out expeditions to try and break the Arab monopoly.

Instead of reaching the coast of China, Columbus landed in the Caribbean. When the natives showed him a pungent fruit, he decided to call it *pimiento*—similar to the Spanish word for black pepper, *pimienta*—for two good reasons. First it had an effect on his tongue that felt like black pepper. But more importantly, Columbus was getting paid to find peppers.

"The land was found to produce much *aji*, which is the pepper of the inhabitants, and more valuable than the common sort black pepper," Columbus wrote in 1493. "The natives deem it very wholesome and eat nothing without it. . . . Fifty caravels might be loaded every year with this commodity."

Not all peppers are created equal. Peppers range in "heat" from the very mild green pepper to the hottest of the hot—the habanero.

The birthplace of the hot pepper was probably central Bolivia, and over the centuries it became the spice most used by Native Americans. Archeological evidence indicates that the natives of Mexico have been using hot peppers for at least seven thousand years. At one point peppers were used to pay taxes to the government. And even after the conquest of Mexico by the Spanish, hot peppers remained a form of tribute. Antonio de Mendoza, the first viceroy of what was called New Spain, demanded dried chilies from the people he conquered.

The Maya, who have lived on Mexico's Yucatán peninsula for at least twenty centuries, eat one of the hottest of all peppers—the habanero.

But the habanero also has a fragrant quality that balances its heat. Amal Naj, author of *Peppers*, believes that the habanero is a symbol of Mayan independence within Mexico.

The habanero is the pepper of choice for the Maya, who were never completely subjugated by the Spanish. They see their pepper as a badge of their self-determination. At the same time they feel that the jalapeño—which is more popular with northern Mexicans—symbolizes the European invader. The majority of habaneros grown in the world are grown in the Mayan territory of the Yucatán, and half of that harvest is eaten right there.

This Mayan mask is from Mexico's Yucatan peninsula, where the world's hottest peppers are grown and consumed.

A PEPPER A DAY...

For thousands of years, hot peppers have been used in Central and South America for their medicinal effects. The Aztecs rubbed peppers on sore muscles. The Maya made a drink of hot pepper, which they used to cure stomach pains, and rubbed hot pepper on their gums to stop toothaches.

When hot peppers were first brought back to Spain by Columbus, they were treated more as a medicine than a spice. During the 1500s, physicians in Seville recommended hot pepper for an assortment of illnesses. Spanish sailors took hot peppers on board their ships to prevent scurvy. Peppers were also thought to improve eyesight.

Albert von Szent-Gyorgyi won the Nobel Prize for Medicine in 1937 for his research on hot peppers.

But the scientific confirmation of hot peppers' medicinal value was first made by Dr. Albert Szent-Györgyi. As the story goes, his wife loved hot peppers and regularly prepared them for dinner. One night, Albert (who was not a fan of hot peppers) took his dinner to his lab so he could *not* eat them without offending his wife. Albert had already isolated the mysterious acid that prevented scurvy, so out of curiosity he studied the peppers' chemical make-up and discovered they were a rich source of the substance, which he called ascorbic acid, or vitamin C. He won a Nobel Prize for his research in 1937.

Recently, scientists in the United States have been studying hot peppers as a possible remedy for the common cold. The capsaicin in hot pepper is chemically similar to the active ingredient in Robitussin. You also find a similar chemical in Sudafed and Vicks Formula 44D. Normally, the mucus in your respiratory system is thin and moves easily through the sinuses. But when you have a cold, mucus becomes thick and stops flowing, coughing begins, and breathing problems develop. The medicines prescribed for these conditions are designed to thin the mucus and get it flowing again. The capsaicin in hot pepper acts in the same way as the medicines.

"Peppers are a food as well as a condiment, a spice, and a medicine," said Dr. Irwin Ziment of the Olive View Medical Center in Los Angeles. "Red peppers and green peppers do contain a lot of carotene, which is a useful aid because it's an anti-oxidant. They also contain several vitamins, the most important being vitamin C. I think many people would be surprised to know that green bell peppers contain more vitamin C than citrus fruits."

It appears that when a concentrated solution of capsaicin is applied to the body it begins to destroy the messengers in the area that signal pain to the brain. And most amazingly, it seems to affect only the pain messengers. The nerves that sense heat, cold, pressure and other sensory messages remain active.

Mexico is the world epicenter of pepper eating. The nation produces a greater variety of peppers than any other country and uses them in the most sophisticated ways. Over 150 different peppers show up on the market and each is used to produce a specific effect within a meal. One variety is the bright green jalapeño, which is used fresh in raw salsas and salads. When mature red jalapeños are smoked and dried, they are known as *chipotles* and used for their intense, rich, and smoky flavor in stews and sauces.

TASTING PEPPERS

It is not just the heat of a pepper that is important to the pungent-pepper lover. The habanero packs a punch but quickly rolls on, leaving a smooth aftertaste. And different peppers impact different parts of the mouth. Since each part of your mouth is sensitive to different tastes, where you get hit is important.

The best way to test your level of tolerance is to start by taking a small bite of the pepper. Then move on until pain brings the experiment to an end.

The hot but fragrant habanero pepper is best tasted one small bite at a time.

Capsaicin is more than one hundred times more pungent than the piperine in black pepper, but unlike black pepper, which inhibits all tastes, capsaicin only blocks the perception of sour and bitter. All other flavor receptors are left intact.

Capsaicin is not soluble in water, so if you can't stand the heat, a cold drink won't help. It does dissolve in alcohol, so one way to get the burning sensation out of your mouth is to rinse with vodka.

An important moment in the history of hot peppers was the signing of the Treaty of Tordesillas in 1494. After Columbus reported the riches of the Caribbean, Portugal and Spain started to elbow for rights to the route. Fearing a war would ensue, Pope Alexander VI drew a longitudinal line through the mid Atlantic, dividing the world in two. The Spanish were given the right to explore and trade in the area to the west; Portugal got everything to the east.

Unhappy with the arrangement, King John of Portugal negotiated the line of demarcation further west, and a new settlement, known as the Treaty of Tordesillas, was reached.

After that longitudinal line was extended around the globe, Spain seized control of the Philippines, while Portugal got the Spice Islands. As a result, it was the Spanish and the Portuguese who spread hot peppers around the world.

Chili peppers are an ingredient in many Mexican dishes, such as this popular bean dip appetizer. Following pages: After the Treaty of Tordesillas in 1494, Spanish and Portuguese explorers spread the hot pepper around the globe.

AQUA

AESTAS

SEPTENTRIO OCEANUS TARTA: RI: CUS

OCEANUS
DEVCALI
DONIVS

MARE

ATLANTI:

CVM

Tropicus Cancri

OCEANUS
Philippinx
In CHINEN
hux
SIS

MARE
ARABICVM et
Golfo de
Bengala
INDI
CVM

RIA

CA

OCEANUS

MAR DI MARE

ÆTHIOPI

BEACH LANTCHIDOL

CVS

Tropicus Capricorni

INDIA TER

RA

AVSTRA

LIS

INCO

NI

GTA

MERIDIES

90

collegistis me · Nudus eram et amici vistis me · Sitivi et dedistis mihi potem · Esurivi et dedistis mihi quod ederem

AER

AVEMS

THE SOURCE OF THE HEAT

In 1876, an English scientist working in India identified the substance in the pepper that was responsible for its heat. Inside the pod and concentrated in the white pith (and sometimes making its way into the seeds themselves) is an odorless, tasteless chemical called capsaicin. But it is not the amount of capsaicin in a pepper that raises the pungency. It is the chemical structure. The shorter the acid chain in the capsaicin molecule, the higher the heat.

Seeding a jalapeno removes the highest concentration of capsaicin, the heat-producing chemical in peppers.

Some authorities believe that hot peppers are addictive, much like caffeine. They theorize that capsaicin hits the nerve endings on your tongue, which sends a message to the brain. The brain thinks the body is under attack and responds by sending out endorphin, a painkiller that produces a pleasurable high similar to a very mild dose of morphine. Every time the pepper lover takes a bite, there's another hit of endorphin.

Columbus was working the Americas for the Spanish, but the Portuguese were also in the field. During the early 1500s, the Portuguese, sailing south along the coast of South America, ran into the hot pepper in Brazil and brought it back to Europe. From there it traveled to Portuguese trading posts in West Africa, around the tip of Africa to India and then to the Portuguese colony of Macao in China. From Macao the pepper hotfooted it with the Portuguese to Japan, the Philippines, and across the Pacific. Within fifty years, hot peppers had traveled around the world.

The Portuguese colony in Macao, China, was the launching point for hot pepper to spread north to Japan and eventually across the Pacific.

Worried about their slaves rebelling, the Portuguese instituted a policy that prohibited any plantation from having a large concentration of slaves from a single tribe or geographical area. One result was that the Portuguese ended up traveling around coastal Africa looking for new sources of slaves, and, as they traveled, they brought along their hot peppers. By the time the British came to dominate the slave trade in the middle of the 1600s, American peppers were so important to Africans that the British included them in their rations onboard the boats that carried slaves to the Americas.

But strangely, when Columbus took his hot peppers back to Europe they were not well accepted. The Turks discovered hot peppers through Indian and Arab traders and introduced them to the Hungarians, who had been conquered by the Turks. Hot pepper quickly became the spice of the poor. The Hungarians loved the flavor of the pepper but not its heat.

During the harvest, workers would remove the veins and seeds of the pepper, where the heat was centered. The pods were dried and ground to a powder, and the result was paprika, which has become the dominant flavor in Hungarian cooking. The microclimate needed for growing the pepper used to make paprika is so specific that only Hungary has been able to produce the highest quality on a commercial scale.

Street traders sell strings of dried hot peppers in Hungary, the country that produces the highest quality commercial paprika. Paprika is made when the dried hot peppers are ground into a powder.

A HELPFUL ADDITIVE

One out of four people worldwide eat hot peppers every day. People cook with hot peppers because they like the taste, but scientists believe that people who enjoy spicy food, especially those who live in hot climates, may well be healthier because of it. Pungent spices like hot peppers, garlic, and cumin are lethal to the microorganisms that cause food to spoil. Over thousands of years without access to refrigeration, people in hot climates developed cuisines that use pungent spices to help preserve food.

In general, poor people eat more hot pepper than the rich. If a diet is based on plain, starchy foods like rice or corn, which is often the case in poor communities, hot pepper will bring flavor to the meal because it has the ability to open the mouth's flavor receptors, making the taste buds more sensitive and food more flavorful.

A woman carries a tray of peppers in the Yucatan peninsula of Mexico. Peppers function as a food preservative as well as a spice in hot climates.

PEPPER PARTICULARS

You can usually tell how far down the evolutionary line a particular pepper is by looking at its size—the smaller it is, the closer it is to its wild ancestor. There are over 1,600 different varieties of pungent peppers, with new forms constantly being developed. Annual rainfall, soil chemistry, and daily temperature patterns affect the development of each species. The peppers grow on plants that are generally two to three feet high. The fruits start out green and color as they ripen.

As a general rule, the hotter the climate a pepper grows in, the more pungent it will be. But it is not just the daily temperature that counts. Long hot nights raise a pepper's pungency. And if a pepper plant is stressed by lack of water or poor soil, its fruits tend to get hotter. Generally, pods that are thin and pointed with tapering shoulders will be more pungent.

In 1912, the pharmacist Wilbur Scoville developed a technique for measuring the heat of a pepper. The Scoville scale ranges from zero for the green bell pepper to 25,000 for the jalapeño to 300,000 for the habanero.

The tapered shape of this ripe red pepper is an indication of the pungent taste within.

Surprisingly, the hot pepper came late to North America. Mexican colonists brought chilies to the American Southwest while African slaves and immigrants from the Caribbean introduced hot peppers to the American South. But most Americans got along without them.

These days, however, pungent peppers in the United States are becoming a hot business. People who had no interest in pungent foods are beginning to try them, and those who already reach readily for the hot sauce want it even hotter. By 1982, hot sauce was already part of the basic rations for American astronauts in space, but astronaut William Lenoir took a fresh jalapeño pepper along on his mission just to play it safe.

TABASCO

The most popular branded use of chili peppers in the world is probably Tabasco Sauce, which is sold in over one hundred countries. It is made on Avery Island, which is a twenty-two-hundred-acre cap that sits on top of a giant salt dome rising up from an ancient seabed about 130 miles west of New Orleans.

In 1862 John Marsh Avery started quarrying the salt and supplying it to the Confederacy, which led the Union Army to invade the island and destroy the salt works' equipment and buildings. When the war was over the Avery family went back into the salt business. This time Edmund McIlhenny, a prominent local banker who had married into the family, began to experiment with making a pepper sauce.

At some point, Edmund had been introduced to tabasco peppers, which had been brought up from Mexico or Central America. Edmund planted the peppers in his garden and used them to add flavor to the monotonous food that was available after the war. Around 1866, he started using the

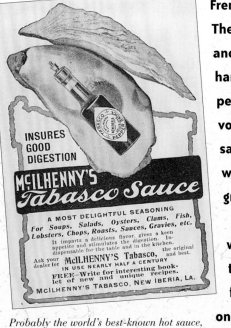

Probably the world's best-known hot sauce, Tabasco Sauce is made from aged red peppers, Avery Island salt, and French wine vinegar—a simple combination that yields the pungent, fiery taste that made it famous.

peppers to make a hot sauce; by 1868 he was selling his creations.

The peppers were crushed, mixed with Avery Island salt, and aged for thirty days in jars or wooden barrels. At that point, French wine vinegar was added. The final blend was aged for another thirty days and regularly hand-stirred throughout that period in order to blend the flavors. Edmund poured the finished sauce into small cologne bottles, which he corked and sealed with green wax.

And that is just about the way it is made today—except today the pepper mash is aged for up to three years instead of only two months. A member of the McIlhenny family still walks the fields and marks the peppers that are ready for harvesting. The pickers spot a ripe pepper by comparing its color to a stick that has been painted with the color of a perfectly ripe pepper. And a McIlhenny examines the mash and decides when it is ready for processing and bottling.

❁

THE STORY OF

Corn

On the fourth day of November 1492, Columbus came ashore on the island now known as Cuba. The natives greeted him with two gifts. One was tobacco, the other was corn. Columbus's diary for the next day contains the following entry:

"There was a great deal of tilled land sowed with a sort of grain-like millet, which they called Mahiz, which tasted very well when boiled, roasted, or made into porridge."

Through Columbus, the American plants of corn and tobacco were introduced to the rest of the world. The Indians presented their corn to Columbus not only because it was a valuable food but also because it was the basis of American civilization.

According to Betty Fussell, author of the book *Crazy for Corn,* "The Indians used it for every possible food and for every possible sacred ceremonial use because corn is at the heart of all the mythology, all the calendars, all the religions, and all the rituals of Mesoamerica. The original word for corn, *mahee* in Arawak, meant seed of life. For the Arawak, because life in the created universe began with corn, with the corn gods, it's really the womb of life. Mother Earth was also Mother Corn, being fertilized by Father Sun. Out of that, the universe sprouts as a corn tree, and all the cobs on that tree are heads of gods.

Corn is a versatile crop—used as a food for both humans and livestock, fuel for automobiles and industry, nearly everyone in the world is touched in some way by corn.

Native Americans taught Pilgrim settlers how to grow corn—and how to survive in the New World.

THE ORIGINAL PACKAGED FOOD

If you check a dictionary you will find that the English word *corn* refers to a country's most important grain. If a country makes its daily bread with wheat, then wheat is described as the "corn" of that country. Oats are the corn of Ireland. Rye is the corn of Sweden.

When the first English speakers arrived in America they saw that maize was the basic food of the natives and so they called it "Indian corn."

Maize is a giant grass that pro-duces very large seeds. Each kernel is really a fruit with an oily seed sur-rounded by starchy nutrients that are held in a hull. The corncob is covered with a husk that makes it easy to har-vest, easy to feed to livestock, and—when dried—easy to transport and easy to store. Corn could be considered one of the original packaged foods.

Corn sounds like the greatest plant on the planet, so what's the hitch? Actually, corn would not be much of anything without outside intervention.

Because the husk is so strong and tight, corn cannot seed itself.

"'We have this unbelievable plant which has all these soft kernels side by side stuck in a cob with a

The corn plant has separate male and female flowering parts. Oddly, the corn plant depends on human assistance in reproduction.

sheath covering them all," relates author Margaret Visser. "They are close together, they are tightly held to the cob, and the sheath cannot be removed by nature. If you let it lie on the ground, it would just simply rot and that's the end of it. Even if you took the sheath off and threw it on the ground, it would not grow. So corn absolutely and totally depends on human beings to survive."

In a healthy cornfield, the plants grow slowly during the day but fast at night. Under ideal conditions a corn plant will grow four and a half inches within twenty-four hours.

Visser explains another corn-growing phenomenon:

"A lot of American farmers have said that they heard their corn growing, and people say, 'Oh, come on.' It's a plant that is very large, and its growth involves unfurling leaves. So if it's growing, a leaf will suddenly unfurl, and it makes a sound, and it scrapes the stalk. You can hear it. In fact, I actually have heard it. It has to be a windless night and it has to be the peak growing sea-son, and you've got to have patience as well—you've got to sit there for a while. But you can hear these unfurling leaves, it's really quite eerie.""

"The corn god is represented in the plant. They also believed that man was created from a dough of corn and blood. So man's life depends wholly on corn, just as corn depends upon man to plant and harvest it."

Before the arrival of the Europeans in America there were no draft animals to help with the farming. Land was cleared by a technique called "slash and burn." The only tools available to slash down the vegetation were sticks or axes and hoes fashioned from wood, seashells, deer antlers, or the shoulder blades of animals. During the 1500s and 1600s, European farmers planted their fields by scattering handfuls of grain over the earth. The grains started growing where they fell. Farmers waited for the weeds to come up with the crop, then pulled up the weeds.

When Europeans got to North America, Central America, and South America, they were astounded at the way the Native Americans practiced agriculture. The Native Americans made little mounds in a checkerboard design along huge fields, miles and miles in extent. And each little mound was exactly in its mathematical place

Peasants worked the land on medieval farms, where corn was sown by scattering grain over the earth.

in rows. The Native Americans planted four or six grains in each mound. A little later they came and planted beans. A little later they planted squash. The corn plant grew straight up, the beans climbed the corn plant, and the squash grew down the mound and covered the space between the mounds to keep down weeds.

The coastal Native Americans planted a fish in every hill. To not add the fish was considered a sin, and without the fish the corn refused to grow. The Native Americans had discovered that corn needed large amounts of fertilizer. The nutrients in the fish helped keep the corn from depleting the soil. Corn, beans, and squash were planted together and eaten together. The Iroquois thought of these crops as the inseparable "three sisters." Indeed, without the addition of beans and squash, a diet of corn is nutritionally incomplete, and the result can be niacin deficiency and an agonizing disease known as pellagra.

When Native American women prepared corn, they often added a little burnt wood or burnt shell to the cook pot.

"This was good in two ways," explains author Margaret Visser. "One, it softened the hulls of the kernels and made it easier to digest. But also it has recently been discovered that alkali loosened this essential vitamin, niacin, so human beings can digest it. And it's extraordinary because the Indians used to offer corn, their sacred food, to the gods. And they never added ash when they offered it to the gods. They somehow knew

that it was human beings who needed the ash. The gods didn't need it."

The Indians of Mesoamerica showed the Spaniards how to grow and store corn. It was a strong plant; it traveled well, grew fast, provided plenty of food; and it quickly spread throughout the world.

"Corn is amazing in that it instantly changed the way the world eats," relates Fussell. "After Columbus's introduction to corn, it went around the world and with great speed developed everywhere it went. Corn grows every place except the North and South Poles. It has this capacity to adapt itself to all kinds of climates and ecologies: damp, dry, high, low. It could be eaten by both men and animals. That's enormously important. Corn has ended up with this double purpose."

Corn grows nearly every place on earth. In Jerusalem, women and boys grind corn in the streets in this photograph from 1880.

When the first English speakers arrived in America they called maize "Indian corn," and were slow to incorporate it into their diets.

Hesitant at first, European settlers to North America eventually incorporated corn into their diet. It was easy to bake corn on a griddle. The result was a firm disc that could be carried on a journey and came to be called journey cakes, which eventually became *johnnycakes*. The corn cake known as pone was a corruption of *oppone*, the Algonquin word for corn batter cooked on hot stones. Whipped egg whites were added to produce a corn soufflé called spoon bread. And coarsely ground white cornmeal was called grits.

But corn was not well accepted in Europe, and many countries never made it part of their diet. The French still think it is only fit for animals, and the Irish rejected it until they were starving. The Italians, on the other hand, embraced corn and used it to make polenta, which is a common dish in northern Italy. It is based on *puls*, or *pulmentum*, the farro, millet, or chick-pea porridge of ancient Rome. Today there are dozens of regional polenta dishes in Italy.

Most of the corn grown in the United States is harvested to feed livestock—cattle, pigs, and chickens.

FEED FOR WHAT FEEDS US

About 85 percent of the corn grown in the United States is used to feed animals. American chickens and cows are fed corn and cornstalks, which means that both meat and milk are part corn. In fact, even the stamp on meat that marks it "grade A" is made with corn oil.

"Columbus's dis-covery of corn in the New World changed the diet of the world. When this kind of fodder became available to animals, it really tipped the balance—in America, where we have all this space for animals—toward a diet of meat replacing grain. We became the giant meat eaters, and that became the model, in a way, for the rest of the world.

American settlers moved west but only as fast as they could plant corn. As America invented itself, it invented more uses for corn. To a considerable extent, the food that a nation eats gives it its identity. Hamburgers and sodas—both of which are only possible because of the proliferation of corn—have turned out to be much more American than apple pie.

During the 1930s and 1940s, the farms of the United States and Canada began to alter their operations so that much of the work could be done by machine. Nowadays, the United States produces more than half of the world's corn, over 250 million metric tons per year. And eighty percent of that crop is grown in the Corn Belt, an area of 350,000 square miles that runs from western Ohio to eastern Nebraska, with the largest tonnage coming from Iowa and Illinois.

Today people cultivate six major

In this photograph from 1907, unmarried Hopi women crush corn for use in cooking.

types of corn: dent, flint, flour, sweet, pop, and waxy. Sweet corn is the variety that is sold in grocery stores on the cob, in cans, or frozen. It is also the type grown in gardens. The oldest variety of corn is popcorn. Flour corn—the basis of the original tortillas and tamales—is rarely grown outside of Central and South America. There, it is still ground by hand. The kernels rest on the metate stone. The hand held *mano* is rolled over them to produce the flour used to make the bread of the Americas. It is still common in much of South and Central America to see the stones placed outside the houses so the neighbors can keep each other company as they work.

Sweet, waxy, and flint corn all have their place in modern industrial agriculture, but the world's most popular corn crop is the starchy variety called dent, which is a reference to the dimpled appearance of each kernel.

Dent corn, so named for its distinctive "dented" appearance, is the world's most popular corn variety.

A country's "corn" is whatever grain is used to make the daily bread—its most important grain. At left, the Mexican tortilla is made with corn, blue corn, or flour. On the following pages, cornbread takes another form in the American South, with its own distinctive style.

POPCORN

Popcorn has a harder hull than other varieties of corn. When it is heated, the starch inside the skin of the popcorn kernel fills with steam until it bursts. With other types of corn the steam leaks out, which is why they do not pop. Some historians believe that the accidental popping of a hard grain in a fire gave ancient humans the idea that cereals were edible.

"You have popcorn beginning as an important American product in New England about 1820 or 1830," explains author of the book *Popped Culture: A Social History of Popcorn in America,* Andrew F. Smith. "And it becomes the celebrity product of this time, with Henry David Thoreau popping corn and writing about it in his journal. And Emerson saying it's a wonderful thing to give to the kiddies at Christmastime; it gets them away from the adults. And you have all these other great Americans talking  about the importance of popcorn, which they all considered to be something new and exciting. So, it enters into America from the top down.

"It is only when the Depression comes that all of a sudden movie owners are confronted with going out of business, or establishing a new revenue stream. And of all snacks, you can make the most amount of money, by far, in popcorn. The profit margin has consistently been 75 percent after all of the other expenses connected with popcorn. So theatre owners found that you either began selling popcorn and snacks or you went out of business. There are nice stories from the 1930s about popcorn making the difference between whether a theatre would survive or not."

The superhero of popcorn was Orville Redenbacher. Orville was an agricultural extension agent in Indiana who came up with a kernel that popped bigger than any kernel ever popped—fifty times bigger than the kernel. Until then, kernels had only popped up to thirty-five to forty times their size.

Orville Redenbacher developed a strain of popcorn that popped bigger than any other brand at that time.

"Popcorn is one of the few foods that's purchased by weight, but sold by volume," explains Smith. "So if you increase the volume, you increase your sales. And, consequently, Orville Redenbacher concluded this was something that was going to revolutionize the popcorn business. So he went out to popcorn processors who sold generic popcorn and tried to convince them that his popcorn was better than theirs. And they all laughed at him.

"And so he decided he was going to prove them wrong. So he really did pile his popcorn into his truck, go around to upscale markets, and gave it away—in Marshall Field's, for instance, in Chicago and other places. And lo and behold, the people loved it.

"So he decided that he needed some marketing help. And he went to a public relations firm in Chicago and paid them $18,000 and said, 'I need help with a name for this stuff.' And after about two-and-a-half hours they said, 'we have the right name for your new popcorn.' And Orville asked, 'What is it?' And they replied, 'Orville Redenbacher's Gourmet Popping Corn.'

"And Orville kind of scratched his head and said, 'Well, my mother thought that was a good name, so therefore it should be a good name for my product, too.' And hence the name Orville Redenbacher's Gourmet Popping Corn was invented. Now, there were no gourmet foods at that time. So this is not obvious today. But in one way, Orville Redenbacher created the market for gourmet food."

In 1726, Jonathan Swift, the author of *Gulliver's Travels*, wrote, "Whoever could make two ears of corn . . . grow upon a spot of ground where only one grew before, would deserve better of mankind, and do more essential service to his country than the whole race of politicians put together."

Native Americans spoke of corn as "She Who Sustains Us," which is as true today as it was before any European set foot on this land. We depend on corn for more than nutrition: from fuel, to plastics, to industrial chemicals, to agribusiness, in many ways our modern technological society is inconceivable without corn. And new uses are invented every year.

*Eighty percent of America's corn is produced in the Corn Belt—
those Midwestern states from western Ohio to eastern Nebraska—
with the largest yield coming from the farmlands of Iowa and Illinois.*

HIDDEN CORN

It is almost impossible to buy anything in an American supermarket that has not been affected by American corn. Frozen fish has a light coating of cornstarch to help prevent it from drying out. All canned foods are bathed in a liquid containing corn. Corn oil is an essential ingredient in soap. Many beers, gins, and vodkas contain corn products. Corn products are used to help foods hold their shape and to prevent ingredients from separating. Every carton, every wrapping, every plastic container is made with corn products.

A key corn product is cornstarch—a white, odorless, tasteless powder that is easily molded. It is used in the production of thousands of products—toothpastes, detergents, match heads, charcoal briquettes.

During the early 1800s, a Russian chemist named G. S. C. Kirchoff found a way to produce sugars by treating cornstarch with acid, and in the process he invented corn syrup. Sweet, easily available, and inexpensive, corn syrup quickly began to replace sugar. The power of sweetness that had belonged almost exclusively to cane sugar was suddenly being shared. Today, corn syrup is used in more products than sugar is—from soda to ketchup.

"Everywhere you look you have corn," explains author Margaret Visser. "You're not aware of it, but underneath it all, it's a driving wheel of the entire American economy. Americans could have used something else for their basic starch; wheat starch or potato starch would have done the job. But in fact, they turned to corn, because they had corn. Corn became essential to modern technological societies all over the world. The technological revolution that took place enabled America to be way out ahead. It gave them a fantastic advantage."

Corn, in the form of cornstarch, corn oil, or corn syrup, is found in almost every product available on the market today.

THE STORY OF
LIVESTOCK
IN AMERICA

When Columbus arrived in the Caribbean, he entered a world that was almost empty of domesticated animals. The people of the Americas had no chickens, no pigs, no horses, and no cattle. In the entire Western Hemisphere, there were only four domesticated mammals and two kinds of fowl.

In 1492, Columbus wrote, "I saw neither sheep nor goats nor any other beast, but I have been here but a short time, half a day; yet if there were any I couldn't have failed to see them. . . . There were dogs that never barked . . . All the trees were as different from ours as day from night, and so the fruits, the herbage, the rocks, and all things."

The llama, the alpaca, the guinea pig, and the Muscovy duck lived in South America. Turkeys could be found in parts of Mexico. Only the dog was widespread. There were no large animals to ride or help with the farming. The Americas were filled with wild game and fish, but it was the domesticated livestock of Europe that changed the way people ate, how they lived and traveled, and even the surface of the land itself.

In the spring of 1493, Columbus made his triumphant return to Spain. Ferdinand and Isabella appointed him to found a mining and agricultural colony on the island of Hispaniola, known today as Haiti and the Dominican Republic.

The modern barbeque evolved from a native Caribbean cooking technique of placing meat on a grating of green twigs over a burning pit.
The smoky taste of a barbequed steak accompanies many backyard, summertime celebrations.

In May of that year he set sail again from Spain. Instead of just the Niña, the Pinta, and the Santa María, he now had seventeen ships, twelve hundred men, ten mares, twenty-four stallions, burros, sheep, and a full complement of cattle and pigs. The animals did well on Hispaniola because the local diseases did not affect them, and there was an unlimited amount of feed and few predators. They reproduced at an extraordinary rate, and within ten years they had taken up residence on most of the Caribbean islands.

That first colony in the Caribbean was considered a failure because the explorers found no gold. But the domestic animals they brought with them ensured the future success of the Spanish colonies in the Americas.

The domestication of animals actually began with the reindeer and the dog about ten thousand years ago. It was not until someone decided to stay put and grow crops that animals were bred in captivity and put to use. Most people assume that humans domesticated animals for economic reasons: cattle for meat and milk; sheep for wool. But that is not the case, according to Professor Emeritus of geography at the University of Vermont Daniel W. Gade:

"If you go back to the archaeological record on some of these animals, you realize

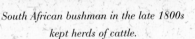

South African bushman in the late 1800s kept herds of cattle.

that they had very important cultic, religious associations. Cattle, for example, were strongly associated in their early stages of domestication with the lunar goddess cult, because of the lunar or moon-like arrangement of their horns, and so they became symbolic for the cult purposes, and as a result of that, they were bred in captivity, as a way of getting more animals for the cult. When you go back to the early domestication of a chicken, you realize that people were not interested in the eggs or the meat, but in the innards, because they would use those innards for divination purposes."

But with the coming of Europeans, this all changed. "There were some domesticated animals here in the Americas, but in fact, most people didn't have much protein," explains Gade. "And so one can argue that the introduction of all of this livestock across the ocean benefited not just the Spanish colonists or the American colonists, the Europeans, but also the native people. This enhanced their health, because the human body gets its protein most efficiently through animal protein."

The pig was first domesticated from the wild boar in what is now Turkey about ten thousand years ago. Pigs have been raised in Spain and Portugal for at least two thousand

Hieroglyphics and inscriptions from ancient Egypt reveal the importance of livestock in Egyptian religious history.

years. After the bull, the pig is the animal most used in Spain's cult rituals.

To a great extent the pig's special place in Spanish society comes from its role as a symbol of Christian identity. For over seven hundred years, beginning in the year 711 and ending with their expulsion in 1492, Muslims occupied Spain. Since Christians ate pork and Muslims did not, eating pork was a way for Spanish Christians to assert their identity. The enormous selection of pork products in Spanish cuisine reflects this historical importance.

Pigs were the first to take on the Americas. They will eat just about anything that is organic and they convert one-fifth of what they eat into food for humans. Spanish conquistadors seeded remote islands by leaving a family of pigs. The pigs would reproduce and be ready for dinner when the next group of Europeans stopped in.

In 1542, a Spanish explorer left a message on an uninhabited island near Río de la Plata:

"In one of the islands of San Gabriel, a sow and a boar have been left to breed. Do not kill them. If there should be many, take those you need, but always leave some to breed."

The first pigs in North America came to Florida from Cuba with Hernando de Soto in 1539. Within three years his original herd of thirteen pigs had become seven hundred.

The pig was a poor man's bank. The farmer could bank on the fact that the little piglet he bought in the spring would be large enough to butcher by late autumn and feed his family during the winter. The remaining pork meat earned enough money to purchase another piglet for the spring, which continued the cycle.

In the Americas, pork was popular from the beginning. Marooned sailors, pirates, and castaways living on the northern beaches of the island of Hispaniola used a native cooking technique that consisted of a grating of green twigs placed over a pit of burning wood that had been dug into the sand. Their pork was cooked on top. The grating was called a *barbacoa*, and the men who used it were called *buccaneers*. Their cooking technique gave us the word *barbeque*.

During the American colonial period, southern hospitality was more about barbecuing a whole piglet over a pit than serving tea. Farmers raised as many pigs as they could because pigs took very little time away from their main crops of cotton and tobacco.

Pigs were a common livestock as well as a Christian symbol for the Spanish. The efficient way pigs convert the food they eat—almost anything—into meat earned them the nickname "poor man's bank."

Today, cattle are raised all over the United States, but the cattle ranching stronghold is west of the Mississippi, where the rainfall is too low for farming and there is no irrigation. Cattle ranching is the major rural activity in at least ten Western states; however, the idea did not originate there.

Southern Spain was the only place in Europe where open-range cattle ranching on horseback was a tradition. Herding on horseback, branding cattle, and driving beef to market were all developed during the Middle Ages by Spanish cattlemen.

The huge open ranges of the pampas, Mexico, Florida, and the western plains of North America were well understood by the Spaniards, who covered them with their cattle and horses. In areas with few natural predators and an endless food supply, the Spainards' livestock multiplied at rates unimaginable in Europe.

Most of the cattle in the Americas from the 1500s to the 1800s were probably at least half wild. Freedom made them fast, lean, and mean—what meat packers call "eight pounds of hamburger on eight hundred pounds of bone and horn." The Texas longhorn, a direct descendant of the Spanish stock, was perfect for the dry conditions of the open range. Without much help from people, it defended itself, lived on little water, and survived the summer heat and winter blizzards. The longhorn were tough and could be driven long distances to the slaughterhouse. But with the coming of the railroads in the 1860s, purebred cattle with a better quality of meat could be shipped to the stockyards. The famed Texas longhorn began to die out.

Ranching was the way the land was used. People were not concerned about owning the land; they just needed to use the grass on the land—the right to graze was the important thing. In the cattle-raising tradition of northern England, land was not owned by individuals; it was set up as a common public area. The English carried the practice to the Americas, and laid out the Boston Commons in 1634 for pasturing cattle. Following the Civil War, some cattle owners had thousands of animals, but not one acre of land. In fact, in the western United States today, most ranching is done on public lands.

The Texas longhorn was once the livestock of choice because of its ability to survive on the open range. However, the meat from a longhorn steer was also tough, and for that reason, it was edged out in favor of other, more tender varieties.

THE NEW LANDSCAPE

European settlers shifted the balance of nature in the Western Hemisphere. Overgrazing by their livestock was probably the single most important factor. The European animals were a threat to the land because horses, cattle, sheep, and goats climbed the slopes and destroyed the fragile network of plants and their roots. Overplowing the soil destroyed the protective ground cover. Erosion occurred on the slopes; trees grew on the savannahs, and weeds and coarse grasses overtook the plains.

As early as 1580, overgrazing in Mexico was apparent. Cattle were starving there in certain areas, as scrub palms took over the open grasslands. When the riches of the grasslands were gone, the increase in herds slowed and in some cases stopped completely. The history of this process is best known in Mexico, but evidence suggests that during the sixteenth and seventeenth centuries, similar problems were occurring throughout the Americas.

With the cattle came the plow, a tool unknown in the Americas. The plow was pulled by oxen. Oxen powered the first sugar mills, transported miners and their equipment into the interior, and brought gold and silver back to the coasts for shipment to Spain.

Since the time of its invention in Mesopotamia some five thousand years ago, the plow allowed farmers in the Middle East and Europe to cultivate huge areas of land. By contrast, the Native Americans used a digging stick for farming, an efficient tool for planting small plots of corn or beans. It was useless, however, for turning over the matted, grassy sod of the plains.

Bringing both cattle and the plow to the Western Hemisphere dramatically altered the landscape and the diet of the Americas. The oxen were strong enough to pull an iron plow across the plains. The plow transformed the grasslands into fields of wheat and corn. Cattle converted unfarmed grassland to food—meat and milk. Native Americans had few animals that gave them this kind of protein.

In South America, cattle were crucial to colonial expansion. The extraordinary amount of meat that came from the cattle farms also made it possible for the Spaniards and their workers to concentrate on mining and not worry about a dependable supply of food.

A yoke of oxen was the way farmers plowed fields until the advent of the tractor revolutionized farm production in the twentieth century.
Following pages: Cowherders in the American West worked in camps tending their herds.

THE AMERICAN COWBOY

Cattle ranching was perfect for the self-image Americans were building. The cattle rancher was an entrepreneur, open to new technologies, attracted by upward social mobility, challenged to make life more efficient. The cowboy, free and independent, became an icon in American folklore, but he picked up his vocabulary and style—everything from bronco to rodeo—from the Spanish. The cowboy represented by John Wayne as part of "real" American culture turns out to have been imported from Spain, the Scottish Highlands, and West Africa.

The Spanish produced breeding herds in the Caribbean and Mexico, and by 1565, on ranches in Florida. Scottish Highlanders and black slaves from West

The lonesome cowboy, popularized by Hollywood and the likes of John Wayne, has become a symbol of the American West.

Africa set up open cattle ranges in the low country of South Carolina. The low-country farmers kept the cattle penned in small common pastures. They herded the animals on foot, using rawhide whips and dogs. In fact, the word "cowboy" is the British word for a cattle herder. Professor of geography Daniel W. Gade explains:

"Remember that song 'Get Along, Little Dogie?' Well, that word *dogie* is believed to have come from West Africa. In Texas, it's used as a name for a small orphaned calf or a steer. Its origin goes back to the Carolina low country, and then ultimately to West Africa. In the Bambara language of West Africa, *dogie* means small. The word *dogie* was brought to the New World, and then to Texas.

During the 1800s, beef started to replace pork as the meat of choice. In Europe steak was expensive—a sign of wealth. Successful immigrants to America ordered prime rib over pork chops as proof of their new status. Beef was touted as a healthy food. Steaks, filets, ribs, roasts, stews—they all became an inexpensive part of the daily diet because of successful cattle ranching. Hamburgers, the chopped beef patty that cooked in minutes and fit perfectly into the American concept of efficient food preparation, became an American phenomenon.

By 1600 meat had become one of the cheapest foods in the Americas; the Spanish–American settlers were probably consuming more meat per person than any other large group of people in the world. In fact, the Europeans in America have rarely experienced any form of famine. For almost five hundred years Americans have been the best-fed people in the world, a fact that has motivated more people to migrate to America than all the religious and ideological forces combined.

Beef, in the form of hamburger or steak, is the meat of choice for many Americans—a fact that has led to the U.S. reputation for being the best-fed country in the world.

During the 1800s, beef started to replace pork as the meat of choice. In Europe steak was expensive—a sign of wealth. Successful immigrants to America ordered prime rib over pork chops as proof of their new status. Beef was touted as a healthy food. Steaks, filets, ribs, roasts, stews—they all became an inexpensive part of the daily diet because of successful cattle ranching. Hamburgers, the chopped beef patty that cooked in minutes and fit perfectly into the American concept of efficient food preparation, became an American phenomenon.

By 1600 meat had become one of the cheapest foods in the Americas; the Spanish–American settlers were probably consuming more meat per person than any other large group of people in the world. In fact, the Europeans in America have rarely experienced any form of famine. For almost five hundred years Americans have been the best-fed people in the world, a fact that has motivated more people to migrate to America than all the religious and ideological forces combined.

Beef, in the form of hamburger or steak, is the meat of choice for many Americans—a fact that has led to the U.S. reputation for being the best-fed country in the world.

THE STORY OF
Cheese

Cheese is one of the oldest of our foods. It probably came into existence as the result of an accident. One theory is that someone in Central Asia or the Near East was carrying milk in a bag made out of the stomach of a calf. The acid in the stomach, known as rennet, caused the milk to separate into liquid whey and solid curds. Then the liquid was drained away and the curds pressed together. The result was cheese.

Food historians tell us that cheese was already being made in 3,000 B.C.—traces of it have been found in ancient Egyptian tombs. In terms of survival, the advantages of cheese over fresh milk are easy to see. It lasts longer than milk without spoiling, it is easy to carry, and it takes up very little space—about one-tenth the volume of the milk from which it was made.

Before the arrival of Columbus in America, there were no cows, no sheep, no goats, and no cheese—the pizza, the cheeseburger, even the nacho had yet to evolve. The livestock that Columbus dropped off in the Caribbean was the first to arrive in this hemisphere. The Spanish used the milk that the livestock produced to make cheese.

Artisanal cheeses are made with individual care and may be made from the milk of cows, goats, or sheep. Specialty cheese making has become a booming new industry in the United States.

At the end of the 1600s, Dominican friars set up a mission in lower California. It was their first settlement on the California coast, and they stocked it with cattle brought from Mexico. During the middle of the 1700s, Franciscan missionaries moved part of the herd north into California and used it to breed hundreds of thousands of cattle, which they used to supply hides and tallow for a large export business.

Capital Dairy in California is one of many dairies that have sprung up in the state. California has overtaken Wisconsin as the new "cheese capital" of the United States.

The first significant demand for dairy products came along with the prospectors who arrived in 1849. Many of the families who rushed west searching for gold traveled across the country with their family cows. When they reached California the men started prospecting; the women started milking the cows and making butter and cheese.

Fresh milk is essential to the quality of cheese. Today, most of the milk produced by American dairy farms is used in the production of cheese.

Finding gold was an iffy business; trading dairy products for gold was very reliable. Successful prospectors paid big bucks for fresh milk, butter, and cheese. The early farmers who supplied them became the nucleus of the California dairy industry.

Today, California has the largest dairy industry in the United States, producing nearly four billion gallons of milk each year. And almost half of that milk goes into the making of cheese. Most of California's dairies are located near the cheese makers. The milk that makes the cheese is usually less than twenty-four hours old, which gives many of these cheeses a fresh milk flavor. The state has about sixty-five cheese makers—some are small artisan operations that hand-make only fifty pounds of cheese per day.

Missions, such as this one in New California, were a center for cheese production, as missionaries had brought the art north from Mexico. Following pages: Monterey Jack cheese, invented in California by David Jacks, is a soft, creamy white cheese that is formed into rounds and aged in racks.

CLASSIC CHEESE MAKING

The process of making cheese starts when the cheese maker adds a starter culture. The culture causes the lactose sugar, which is found naturally in milk, to turn into lactic acid.

Rennet is added, which causes the proteins in the milk to clump together, forming curds. The solid curd mixture is cut up and the liquid whey is drained off. Larger curds usually produce a softer and moister cheese.

If the cheese being made is a cheddar-style cheese, the curds will be cheddared, which means that blocks of curd will be piled on top of one another and pressed together, then piled on top of one another again, and pressed again. The cheddaring process releases the liquid whey; the result is a semi-firm, dry cheese with a fine texture.

To get a totally different type of cheese, the curds are cooked and stirred, which turns the clumps of protein molecules into strands. The texture of a string

cheese or mozzarella is the result of the curds being cooked.

After cooking, the cheese is salted. Salt slows down the action of the starter bacteria and draws additional moisture out of the cheese. The net effect is to retard the aging process, giving the cheese time to develop.

The curds are put into a form to give the cheese its shape. Some are pressed to take out more whey, which yeilds a firmer cheese. Some are not pressed, which results in a softer cheese.

At this point, the cheese is ripened in a storage room where the temperature and the humidity can be controlled. The cheeses are turned regularly to redistribute the butterfat, which tends to sink to the bottom.

Letting wine sit around in barrels is a form of ripening—of controlled aging. Letting cheese sit around in a ripening room is also a form of controlled aging.

Cheese curds are formed at the start of any cheese-making process. It is the size and treatment of these curds that determines the type of cheese produced from them. The cheese curds are put in molds to form the round shape for aging.

The Marin French Cheese Company opened in the San Francisco Bay area in 1865, which makes it the oldest continually operated cheese company in the United States. They started by supplying cheese to bars. Bar cheese was given free to people when they ordered a drink—like pretzels or nuts today. These days Marin French is well known locally for its soft-ripened cheeses like Brie and Camembert.

Milk is delivered to the cheese factories daily. Today most cheese is made from milk less than twenty-four hours old.

Other California cheese makers have major facilities. Hilmar is the largest cheese making complex in the world. It was put together by twelve local dairy producers in 1984. The founders were simply trying to find a use for the milk they were producing on their farms.

Hilmar makes cheddar, Colby, Monterey Jack, Parmesan and mozzarella—and they make one million pounds of cheese every day.

The counties just north of San Francisco make up the oldest dairy district in the state, with an environment that is perfect for dairying. The cool ocean air and fog that come in off the Pacific give the region an even temperature throughout the year, and the soil is ideal for the clovers and grasses that feed dairy cattle. The long rainy season lengthens the time that the cattle can feed on natural pasture.

The mother of the California cheese industry was Clarissa Steele. Originally from New England, she came west with a family recipe for making cheddar. The recipe had traveled across the Atlantic with her ancestors and was based on milk from easy-going English dairy cows. The cattle that surrounded Clarissa's farm, however, descended from old Spanish herds that had come up from Mexico— herds that were not accustomed to being milked. A ranch hand roped a cow for her and eventually she was able to milk it. The cheese Clarissa made inspired her husband and three cousins to go into the cheese business. During the 1850s the "Steele Brothers" became the first commercially successful cheese producers in California.

DAIRY MAIDS

In England, there was a traditional division of labor in dairying. Men would herd the sheep, goats, and cows, while women did the milking and made the butter and cheese. In colonial America, making cheese became a skill that was passed from mother to daughter, and selling their cheese gave farmwomen an independent source of income. Rural women also set up small factories to produce cheese for urban markets. The profits from these enterprises helped cheese-making families educate their daughters.

The "milkmaid" was responsible for drawing milk from cows for drinking and for cheese making.

After the Civil War, cheese factories expanded to produce cheese for the growing American cities. The factories required both capital and unskilled heavy labor, which meant that men rather than women went into the business. Ultimately, the small-scale producers could not compete with inexpensive industrial cheeses.

In the past thirty years American women have started small cheese-making companies that offer a superior product, revitalizing the artisan cheese-making tradition. Today, women play prominent roles in many dairies.

Cheese and butter makers along the coast had been sending their products to San Francisco by boat. But the unreliable schedules, temperature changes, salt air, and shipboard moisture made the operation a tricky one. So most dairy products stayed in the neighborhoods where they were made.

The exception was the cheese made by David Jacks. During the 1870s, Jacks acquired over sixty thousand acres of land in Monterey and the Salinas Valley. He also bought fourteen dairy farms in Monterey and nearby Big Sur. In partnership

Cheese makers in Jack Cheese factories use an old recipe that originated in California missions.

with Swiss and Portuguese dairymen, he dominated the dairy business throughout Monterey. Jacks was able to get his buddies in the railroad business to run a line from Monterey to San Francisco so he could make regular cheese shipments by train.

Jacks's cheese was soft, white, and based on an old California Mission recipe. He marked the outside of his shipping crates "Jacks, Monterey." During the 1880s, his cheese became so popular that it was asked for by name—usually as "Jacks cheese from Monterey." But it was easier to call it Monterey

Jack. Some folks consider it to be the most important cheese created in the United States.

During World War I, Monterey Jack took on a second form. A San Francisco cheese wholesaler left a surplus shipment of Monterey Jack sitting in his warehouse. When he finally found it and opened the crates, he discovered that the cheese had aged quite nicely. It had lost most of its moisture and was as hard as Parmesan or Romano. It had also acquired a nutty flavor. The war had cut off his supply of cheese from Italy and the large Italian community in San Francisco needed a replacement. Dry Jack was quickly accepted by Italian-American cooks.

California's great Central Valley runs between the foothills of the Sierra Nevada on the east and the Coast Range on the west. It is about four hundred miles long and forty to sixty miles wide.

California farmland and dairy cows help make California the prime dairy region it is today.

During the 1870s, William Chapman, one of the largest landowners in the state, sold eighty thousand acres of Central Valley to a group of German settlers and encouraged them to grow alfalfa. The crop was so successful that it became the primary feed for the dairy industry in central and southern California. By 1910, the Central Valley had become the state's principal dairy region.

During the early 1990s, in a surprise upset, California took the title of top milk-producing area in the United States. In previous years, that honor had gone to Wisconsin, traditionally known as the "Dairy State." Dairymen and dairywomen flocked to California to take advantage of inexpensive land and a year-round temperate climate. To boost the area's economy, cheese makers have started making high-end products. Their goal is to end up being to cheese what Napa Valley is to wine.

FARMSTEAD PRODUCERS

There are fewer than a dozen farmstead cheese producers in California. Farmstead cheese is made on the farm site using only milk from the herd located on that farm.

A good example of a small farmstead producer is Three Sisters Farmstead Cheese. The sisters are Marisa, Lindsay, and Hannah Hilardes. Marisa and her father Rob decided that they needed to do more with the milk from their herd and attended a series of classes presented by California Poly-technic State University in San Luis Obispo. With their formal training completed, they began pro-duction. Within a year their Serena Cheese, which is a cross between Parmesan and aged Gouda, won a silver medal at the World Cheese Awards.

North of San Francisco is the Point Reyes Farmstead Cheese Company. Bob Giacomini wanted to reduce the size of his dairy herd but not his income. He was also looking for a way to bring his daughters back to the family farm. He accomplished both objectives, and in the bargain produced California's first blue cheese.

Farmstead cheese producers, such as Farmstead Cheese Company in California are producing quality cheeses from the farmstead's own dairy cows.

The southern California coastal region, starting in Los Angeles and running south to San Diego, has a couple dozen cheese makers. Here, for several decades, Jules Wesselink has been a successful dairy farmer with a herd of Holsteins. In 1996, he decided to begin making cheese from his herd's milk. He is of Dutch descent and went back to Holland to learn the tradi-tional Dutch techniques for making Gouda cheese. When he returned, he convinced his daughter and her husband to become cheese makers. They produce a farmhouse Gouda that is offered at several stages of ripeness, as well as Goudas flavored with cumin, jalapeño peppers, or herbs.

The cattle that Columbus brought over introduced the idea of dairying in the Ameri-cas. And today, dairies in the United States are making cheeses that match the quality of the great cheeses of Europe.

Whether cut straight from a wheel of smoked Gouda or melted in the popular grilled cheese sandwich, cheese is enjoyed in many forms throughout the world.

⚓

MEDITERRANEAN
FOODS IN THE AMERICAS

As Columbus outfitted his ships, he kept in mind the possibility that he and his men might end up stranded in a strange land without access to familiar foods. He had visited Portugal's colonies in West Africa and knew that foods from home might be essential to his survival.

The Niña, the Pinta and the Santa María were stocked with water, biscuits, salted pork and beef, dry salted cod, sardines and anchovies, dried chickpeas, raisins, olive oil, vinegar, and fortified wine—typical provisions for Spanish ships of the period and typical of the diet of people living on the northern coast of the Mediterranean Sea.

The Mediterranean is the place where Europe, Africa, and Asia intersect—the place where people from different cultures meet and exchange ideas, goods, and food. It was the center of the classical world—ancient Greece, Rome, Egypt, Carthage—they were all Mediterranean cultures, and the local cuisine has always been a synthesis of ingredients and cooking styles.

As Spanish and Portuguese colonists settled in the Americas the foods they brought with them from the Mediterranean were blended with the foods available in the Americas. Lacking European-style bakeries, the cooks of Mexico adapted the tortilla by making it with wheat as well as corn. Olive oil, cheese, garlic, and onions from the Mediterranean took up residence next to American foods like corn, chili peppers, tomatoes, and chocolate. Today's Mexican cooking owes as much to the Mediterranean diet of 500 years ago as it does to the kitchens of the Maya and Aztecs.

Popular Mediterranean appetizers include hummus, tabbouleh, stuffed grape leaves, and varieties of seafood and shellfish.

By the end of the 1800s, West Coast farmers were turning California into a second Mediterranean, but most of the cooking in the United States was still inspired by the British—minimal amounts of seasoning, very few vegetables, lots of meat and potatoes.

Major variations in diet were usually the result of food fads, health-food movements, and ideas promoted by the emerging schools of dietary science and home economics. The majority of American cooking was excruciatingly boring.

The event that began to alter gastronomy in the United States was the arrival of millions of European immigrants—particularly those from Italy. At first, nutritionists from the federal, state, and city governments tried to convince the Italians that their traditional diet was unhealthy. Cooking classes were set up to teach the immigrants how to prepare foods in the bland, uninteresting

Italian dishes are included in what we consider Mediterranean cooking. Italian immigrants in America added meat to their pasta dishes, creating an Italian-American favorite, spaghetti and meatballs.

style that had become the dominant form for American cooks. Fortunately, the Italians held on to their diet and in doing so saved American cuisine. They added a little more meat to their meals and even invented spaghetti and meatballs. But, for the most part, they ate what they had been accustomed to eating back in Italy.

They imported pasta and olive oil from Italy and built networks of distributors to make sure that Italian immigrants across the country could have access to Italian ingredients. They started farms and backyard gardens to supply the produce they wanted.

When World War II came to an end, tens of thousands of servicemen who were stationed in Italy returned to the United States with a great appreciation of Italian cooking. By that point there were large Italian communities in many American cities, particularly in the Northeast and in San Francisco. Good Italian food was easily accessible and became more and more popular during the 1950s.

During the 1970s, Mediterranean food in the United States became even more popular. It is hard to point to a single reason for the shift, but one important element was the dramatic increase in the number of Americans traveling to Italy—Rome had become the most popular destination for American tourists. In Italy, they were learning about dishes with complex flavors, real pasta, good wine, good bread, and the use of olive oil instead of butter. Back in the United States, gourmet shops were opening in major cities and offering a vast collection of imported Italian foods. European-style bakeries were springing up.

In addition, there was a major new wave of immigrants from the Mediterranean, and this time they were not primarily from Italy—they were from Greece, Turkey, Lebanon, Palestine, and Egypt. They built communities that retained many of the aspects of their homeland, especially when it

came to food. Slowly but surely, average Americans were introduced to these foods and eventually came to accept them as part of their diet. They were new to the United States, but among the oldest foods in Western cookery.

By the early 1990s, the traditional foods of the Mediterranean had a widespread appeal in America that was suddenly enhanced when a series of scientific papers claimed that the Mediterranean diet could reduce chances of heart disease and cancer.

The Mediterranean is so large and encompasses so many cultures that it is difficult to simply define a Mediterranean cuisine. However, Portugal, Spain, France, Italy, and Greece share a history in which three foods have been constant—wheat bread, olive oil, and wine—none of which existed in the Americas prior to the arrival of Columbus. All three were central to the diets of the ancient world.

Oregano is a plant native to the Mediterranean. The spice derived from this plant is heavily used in Italian cuisine—especially tomato sauces. Surprisingly, oregano is a little used spice outside of Italian cooking, even among the countries of the Mediterranean.

OLIVE OIL

Olive trees can live for hundreds of years, and their roots are so deep that even if the tree is cut down, its roots will survive and send out new growth. As a result, the olive tree became a symbol of regeneration, immortality, and dependability.

The technological skill necessary to cultivate an olive tree, make the olives edible, and produce olive oil is so complex that the ancient Greeks used "olive knowledge" as a criteria for judging a society's ability to function. The cultivation and production of olive oil meant that the society was living in a state of relative harmony, because the demands of processing were so intensive that they generally occurred only in more or less peaceful times.

For many centuries, olive oil harvesting and processing were done by sailors in winter, when tough weather kept them on shore. Olive production became their winter work, and reinforced the olive as a symbol of home, safety, and the security of a peaceful,

In the Biblical story of the Great Flood, Noah let go a dove to bring back signs of dry land. The olive branch it returned with has come to symbolize peace and renewal.

smoothly running society. When one of the doves that Noah sent out to search for land returned with an olive branch in its beak, the signs of peace and eventual regeneration were blended into one symbol.

Because olive oil gives off very little smoke when it burns and burns very slowly, it was used in lamps that were part of religious rituals. It came to symbolize the feeding of the body and the soul. Throughout biblical times it was used as an anointment and later in the coronation ceremonies of the kings and queens of Europe.

Countries that border the Mediterranean use olive oil in their cooking and are the major producers of the olive oils presently used in the Americas. In many parts of the Mediterranean, you can still see the most traditional method of production. The olives are brought in from the fields, the leaves and stems are removed, and they are washed and transported to the press.

The pressing is done by stone wheels that each weigh a little over two thousand

The olive tree requires a long, hot growing season to ripen the fruit. Ripe olives range in color from green to copper brown to a blackish purple.

pounds. The wheel crushes both the meat and the pits of the olive, reducing them to a thick paste. The paste is spread on disks made of hemp that are placed onto a spindle. When the column of discs is about five feet high, it is moved to a machine that applies an enormous amount of pressure, squeezing out the olive's dark juice and oil. The mixture of juice and oil goes into a piece of equipment that separates the olive juice from the extra virgin olive oil. The oil is then filtered and bottled.

In Mediterranean cooking, olive oil is an essential ingredient of everyday foods.

Olive oil is the most universal of the ingredients in Mediterranean cooking. Islamic cultures avoid wine and in parts of the Middle East pasta and couscous are favored over wheat bread, but every culture in the Mediterranean uses olive oil.

In the United States, Thomas Jefferson, always ready for a gastronomic experiment, planted olive trees on his estate in Virginia, but the results were poor. Southern planters were not interested, and soon the idea of an olive and olive oil industry along the southeast coast dried up. However, Jefferson's love of Mediterranean food remained intact as evidenced by the fact that he imported an Italian pasta-making machine and put it to regular use.

But North America's interest in the olive goes back for at least a hundred years before Jefferson. Franciscan friars had been cultivating small olive groves in Mexico, and when they moved north into California they brought their olive-growing technology with them. Their first successful harvest of "mission olives" in North America was in San Diego during the mid-1700s. From then on the Spanish missions along the coast of California were in the olive business, though on a small scale.

After the United States annexed California, agriculturists began to cultivate California olives on an industrial scale. They planted the olive trees next to their vineyards and by the 1880s were producing olives and olive oil of the highest quality. Napa and Sonoma counties above San Francisco proved to have perfect olive-growing conditions.

During the early years of the twentieth century, many California farmers turned to the cultivation of table olives as opposed to olives for oil. While most the world's olive crop is crushed for oil, much of California's production goes straight onto pizzas, or into salads and martinis.

A mixture of gin and vermouth, the martini is usually completed with the olive.

WHEAT BREAD

Wheat, oats, barley, and rye contain a complex of proteins known as gluten. When gluten combines with water it produces a sticky substance that makes bread dough malleable and traps the gases released into the dough from the yeast. Wheat is the grain with the most gluten and is therefore the logical choice for making leavened bread.

Wheat bread has had an honored place in the history of Western cuisine for thousands of years. The word "companion" is Latin for someone with whom you share your bread. In medieval and Renaissance Europe the type of bread you ate defined where you stood in society.

Mediterranean pita bread is made from wheat flour.

A crusty white loaf similar to what you find today in Italy and France was the daily staple of the upper classes. The poor made their bread from rye, millet, or oats.

Wheat bread was the only form of bread approved by the Catholic Church for use in the Eucharist. When early colonists were unable to grow wheat successfully in the Caribbean or the coastal parts of Mexico, more conservative members of the church became concerned that the New World was the devil's world. They believed that God would not have created a place in which the essential elements of the Eucharist could not be produced.

As colorful as it is flavorful, the Mediterranean table spread, shown on the following page, is even more enjoyable with an ocean view.

VEGETABLES

Upper-class Europeans living in the Mediterranean valued beef and game as much as their counterparts to the north, but Mediterranean cooks have always had a greater interest in vegetables than their northern neighbors. Salad greens were far more common in the diet of Renaissance Italians than they were for people living in northern Europe.

To a certain extent the Mediterranean interest in vegetables was a result of the intense seagoing commercial traffic within the area.

Southern European ports had centuries of contact with the Ottoman Empire—Arab, Persian, and Turkish cooking often favors vegetables over meat. During the seven hundred years that the Moors controlled most of Spain, they introduced spinach, zucchini, artichokes, cucumbers, melons, rice, eggplant, and citrus fruits. Much of what we consider southern European cooking originated in the Arab world.

SEAFOOD

Because of the easy access to the sea, Mediterranean communities had a great appreciation of fish and seafood. The dominant religion in Mediterranean Europe was Catholicism. And at the time, the Catholic calendar had 166 fast days, when meat was not to be eaten. If you could afford them, fish and seafood became the protein source during fast periods. The poorer groups in society turned to legumes—fava beans, peas, or chickpeas—for their fast days.

Linguine with seafood is just one of the many Mediterranean recipes that show the region's great appreciation for the fruits of the sea.

DAIRY

Dairy products were the most widely used foods derived from animals. Yogurt was a mainstay in Middle Eastern cooking. And cheeses were popular in the southern European countries. One distinct advantage cheese had over other milk products was its longer shelf life, which made it particularly useful to sailors who could not carry fresh milk aboard ship.

FRUIT

Dates have been a staple food in Mediterranean cultures for thousands of years and may very well be our oldest cultivated fruit. Sculptures that are at least seven thousand years old clearly show Middle Eastern farmers working with date palms. Spanish monks brought date palms to the Americas and eventually grew them in their California missions.

Date palms come in pollinating male and fruit-producing female forms. Natural pollination would require that farmers reserve half of their land for male trees that do not produce fruit, so date growers do their pollinating by hand and have done so for thousands of years.

The Mediterranean-like climate of part of California, make the state an ideal location for the production of fruits such as dates, oranges, limes, and lemons.

Because of their sweetness—a dried date can have seventy percent of its weight in sugar—dates have often been thought of as nature's candy. Today, California is a major producer of dates.

Franciscan monks also experimented with citrus orchards, planting groves of oranges, limes, and lemons. During the late 1840s, Anglo settlers rediscovered the mission orchards and by the end of the 1800s, southern California was a major center for citrus production, exporting oranges to the rest of the United States. The crates in which the oranges were shipped featured elaborate labels depicting idyllic West Coast landscapes and did much to create the popular image of California as a land of endless summers.

THE STORY OF
Coffee

The most famous story about the discovery of coffee takes place in Ethiopia. It tells of a goat herder who noticed that after his goats ate the berries of a certain bush, they became energized. The goat herder tasted the berries and they had the same effect on him. A local monk joined in the experiment and ended up in a similar state of excitement. The berries became a regular part of the diet at the nearby monastery and were considered a gift from heaven because they helped keep the brothers awake during their evening prayers.

The nomadic people of what is now Ethiopia have been using the fruits, seeds, and leaves of the coffee tree for more than one thousand years. But it was not a major part of their diet, and they did not make what today is thought of as coffee. They used the leaves and the dried husks of the berries to make a tea-like drink. They also crushed the seeds of the plant and rolled them into balls with animal fat, creating a mentally stimulating fast food that could be carried on long journeys.

The word *coffee* comes from an Arabic word for wine. Islamic law forbids wine's consumption, and in many ways the Islamic world has chosen coffee to take its place. As early as the tenth century, Arabian doctors were using coffee as a medicine, but its first serious cultivation as a cash crop took place in Yemen during the 1400s. Religious pilgrims visiting Mecca spread the news about coffee throughout the Arab world, and coffeehouses soon became part of every Islamic community.

The first step toward making the perfect cup of coffee is choosing the right bean. Processed coffee beans vary in flavor and color, depending on the method and timing of the roast.

At first, its adoption was questioned by conservative scholars who argued that coffee should be treated as wine and prohibited. But coffee's intoxicating effects were the opposite of wine's, and a much larger group of Koranic scholars defended the beverage.

They were enthusiastic about coffee's ability to sharpen the mind, loosen the tongue, and keep a person awake through long hours of study. By the early 1500s, shops where coffee could be bought and shared were opening all over Arabia.

BREWING A REVOLUTION

A Dutch traveler described Middle Eastern coffeehouses as "large halls, with floors that are covered with straw mats. At night the rooms are lit with lamps. The customers are served with smoking pipes and cups of coffee. Scholars sit in these establishments and tell tales, deliver speeches on various subjects and receive small contributions from the audience for their efforts." A French traveler pointed out that "the guests mingle without distinction of rank or creed"—everyone talked to everyone.

The Middle Eastern coffeehouse has been a traditional place to share ideas and exchange news and information.

The caffeine in coffee is a stimulant, and in these ancient Arab coffeehouses it stimulated original thought, a sense of freedom, and a desire to discuss politics and social change. In a world without newspapers and magazines, radio or television, coffeehouses quickly became centers for travelers and locals to exchange news, stories, and opinions. The ruling classes, however, were threatened by this development.

In 1511, opposition to the administration of Khair Beg, the mayor of Mecca, was a common subject of conversation in the coffeehouses. The mayor was so offended by these public discussions that he tried to close the coffeehouses and ban all coffee drinking. But local public opinion and the view of his coffee-loving superiors in Cairo made the ban short lived.

The role of the coffeehouse as a gathering place for revolutionaries and a center for social unrest continued as part of coffee's history—plans for both the French Revolution and the American Revolution were discussed and developed during meetings that were held in coffeehouses.

When the Turks occupied Yemen in 1536, they learned about coffee and coffeehouses and brought both back to Constantinople. Coffee, and public coffeehouses, became so popular among the Ottomans that by the end of the 1500s, European visitors to Constantinople reported that there were six hundred coffeehouses in the city and that they served the same function as the taverns in Europe.

The Ottoman Turks controlled Europe's trade with the Arab world, introduced coffee to Europe, and were the first to make coffee a commodity. They guarded their coffee monopoly and forbade any shipment of fertile coffee fruit to their European or Asian customers. But during the early 1600s, a Muslim pilgrim from India taped a few seeds to his chest, returned home without having them discovered, and started a coffee farm in Mysore. He did not have much commercial success, but he did prove that it was possible to grow coffee outside of the Middle East.

In 1616, a Dutch trader managed to smuggle a coffee tree out of the Yemeni port of Aden, and by the 1650s the Dutch were growing coffee commercially in Ceylon. During the early 1700s, the Dutch East India Company dominated the world coffee markets with harvests from its coffee plantations in Java. And each year Europe's demand for coffee expanded.

Coffeehouses, such as the one depicted here on Bride Lane, Fleet Street in London, were a center for heated debate in England.

Coffee arrived in Europe at the same time as two other hot, caffeinated drinks—chocolate from the Americas and tea from East Asia. All three were generally accepted by the upper classes. They were less successful with the rest of the population, who were accustomed to drinking beer with breakfast.

But Europe was beginning a cultural transformation, and as European society modernized, coffee became the drink of choice for the emerging middle class. The first coffeehouses in Europe served the same function they had in the Arab world; they provided a place for scholars, artists, journalists, and political activists to socialize, to do business—and to make plans for changing the world.

COFFEE PREPARATION

In Turkey and Arabia, coffee had been brewed by repeatedly boiling ground coffee in a brass or copper pot called an *ibrik*. It was served (as it still is today) along with the grounds. Early European drinkers adopted a similar method. But by the early 1800s, various drip coffee methods were being devised, and a primitive form of filtered coffee evolved. It required wrapping the grounds in a cloth bag before boiling them in water, but it worked.

Napoleon, set on making France self-sufficient, recommended that his people turn to the roasted root of the chicory plant as a coffee substitute. While chicory did not succeed as a substitute, it did become popular as a coffee extender, and French coffee drinkers developed a taste for coffee with chicory that they passed on to their American colonists. The taste is still popular in New Orleans.

By the turn of the twentieth century, Europe was a hotpot of coffee innovation. In 1901, Italian inventor Luigi Bezzera built a steam-driven machine that could make single cups of coffee to order—and espresso was born. Espresso and the espresso bar, operated by a knowledgeable *barista*, became popular throughout Italy, and after World War I, quickly spread across the Continent.

In 1908, Melitta Bentz, a German housewife, tired of scooping grounds out of her coffee, came up with a drip coffeemaker lined with blotter paper and invented modern filter coffee. For the rest of the century, northern Europeans and Americans would drink filtered coffee, while southern Europe remained loyal to espresso.

One of the many ways to prepare coffee is with a French press.

In the early decades of the 1600s, coffee became a fad among English college students, and in 1650 a group of students at Oxford opened the first coffeehouse in Europe. In 1652, Pasqua Rosée, an Armenian immigrant, opened the first coffeehouse in London. It was an instant success, and within fifty years coffeehouses had cropped up all over the city. They were a hit with writers, artists, and critics and were commonly known as "penny universities," under the theory that a person could sit in a coffeehouse and, for the price of a cup, get an education.

Up to the 1600s, most of what we think of as big business was done by governments—most small businesses were run out of people's homes. The coffeehouses provided homes away from home for a new breed of capitalists, who were busy building private industry. Lloyd's of London, until recently the largest insurance company in the world, began life in 1688 as a coffeehouse, which just happened to be popular

The espresso coffee machine makes one or two cups of coffee at a time by quickly forcing hot water through the grounds.

with insurance brokers. Other coffeehouses gave rise to holding companies, stock exchanges, and newspapers. In England, the coffeehouse became known as the place where businessmen did business.

It was a time when many people were beginning to question the divine right of kings, and the coffeehouse became the popular spot to ask and answer those questions. Several European leaders, including Frederick the Great of Prussia, banned coffeehouses as hotbeds of sedition, but, as the mayor of Mecca had found out four hundred years earlier, even a royal edict is no match for the public's love of coffee.

In 1674, a Women's Petition Against Coffee was published in London. It claimed that coffeehouses kept men from their homes and made them sexually impotent. The following year, King Charles tried to close the coffeehouses with a proclamation:

"Whereas it is most apparent that the multitude of Coffee Houses of late years set up and kept within this kingdom, and the great resort of idle and disaffected persons to them, have produced very evil and dangerous effects; and that many tradesmen and others, do herein misspend much of their time, which might and probably would be employed in and about their Lawful Calling and Affairs; and that in such houses . . . divers false, malicious and scandalous reports are devised and spread abroad to the Defamation of his Majesty's Government, and to the Disturbance of the Peace and Quiet of the Realm; his Majesty hath thought it fit and necessary, that the said Coffee Houses be put down, and suppressed."

The public outcry in response to this proclamation was so great that it was withdrawn within eleven days. Coffee and free speech won the day.

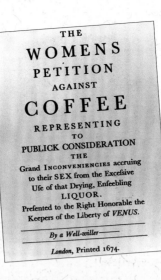

THE
WOMENS
PETITION
AGAINST
COFFEE
REPRESENTING
TO
PUBLICK CONSIDERATION
THE
Grand Inconveniencies accruing
to their SEX from the Excessive
Use of that Drying, Enfeebling
LIQUOR.
Presented to the Right Honorable the
Keepers of the Liberty of VENUS.
——— By a Well-willer———
London, Printed 1674.

Insurance giant Lloyd's of London had humble beginnings as a coffeehouse.

HYPERACTIVE INGREDIENT

German poet Johann Wolfgang von Goethe—who was struggling to kick a lifelong coffee addiction—was an amateur scientist as well. Curious about the power the bean had over him, Goethe, whose portrait is shown at right, asked a young chemist, Friedlieb Ferdinand Runge, to do a chemical analysis. In 1819, Runge—who went on to become an important figure in the history of chemistry—came up with the answer when he isolated crystals of pure caffeine.

By the late 1800s, coffee had become an established drink throughout the world, but because of its caffeine content some people were beginning to have concerns about its effect on good health. In 1906, Ludwig Roselius, a German coffee merchant, found a way to extract caffeine from coffee beans. Roselius's coffee was a success, and the brands he established, Kaffe Hag and Sanka, are still around.

The acceptance of coffee on the European continent did not take place as quickly as it had in England. In France, coffee was nowhere until 1669, when Ottoman ambassador Suleiman Aga's arrival in Paris sparked a wave of Turkomania—leading to the establishment of *cafés* all over the country.

In Germany and Austria, where beer drinking was a matter of national pride, there was heavy resistance to the new drink. The event that began to change Austria's attitude was the siege of Vienna in 1683. The city was attacked and surrounded by a Turkish army. Eventually, the siege was broken and the Turks retreated, leaving behind hundreds of sacks filled with coffee beans.

A postcard from the market place in Vienna, Austria, shows a place where a nation's love of coffee began.

Coffee was a regular part of the Turkish diet, but was almost unknown to the Viennese. A war hero named Franz Kolschitsky, however, had seen how the Turks brewed coffee. He brewed the beans and served his Viennese guests their first cups of coffee. As a reward for his wartime efforts, he was given a building, which he turned into the city's first coffeehouse—the model for Vienna's great gastronomic landmarks. The coffeehouse, as a Viennese patron once said, was the "ideal place for people who want to be alone but need company for it."

The coffeehouse played its part in the Age of Enlightenment, the 1700s, a time when philosophers believed in the reasonable mind of man, in natural law, and in universal order.

They promoted a rational and scientific approach to religious, political and economic issues, and attacked the social restraints and censorship of the time. The idea of man as an essentially rational being set the stage for the economic policies of Adam Smith and the political ideas of Thomas Jefferson and Benjamin Franklin. And it was in coffeehouses that many of these social, economic, and political concepts were first presented and discussed.

By the middle of the 1700s, there were tens of thousand of coffeehouses throughout Europe. More and more people were moving from the countryside into the cities. Coffee, both social and sobering, proved to be the perfect drink for Europeans as they entered the modern world. And they wanted more and more of it all the time.

Eager to capitalize on the demand for coffee, European entrepreneurs were always on the lookout for new sources of the bean. The Dutch, like the Turks before them, did their best to prevent other interests from getting their hands on live coffee plants. But in 1723, a French officer, Gabriel Mathieu de Clieu, smuggled a single coffee plant across the Atlantic and planted it in Martinique in the West Indies—the first coffee plant in the Americas, and probably the parent of most of the coffee grown in the world today.

BEAN BASICS

Traditionally, coffee had been made from a variety of the bean known as *arabica*. It was the plant that was first discovered in Ethiopia, cultivated in Yemen and spread around the world by European coffee traders. But arabica matures slowly, will only grow properly at high elevations, and is susceptible to disease. At the beginning of the 1900s, a variety known as *robusta* was found in the African Congo. It was a much tougher plant, able to grow in a wider range of environments, and it packed twice the caffeine punch of arabica. The taste was not up to the standard set by arabica, but the economics of using robusta were too great for the coffee producers to ignore.

Consumers in the United States became accustomed to the harsher taste of the new beans. So did the Europeans, although the French and Italians developed much darker roasts in order to compensate. The large manufacturers began to put together blends in pursuit of the perfect coffee. They would pick one for acidity, one for body, one for flavor, and so on. In the process, a new breed of coffee-tasting expert was born. In a procedure called "cupping," pioneered by a few San Francisco coffee traders in the early 1900s, tasters brewed weak infusions of barely roasted beans, and slurped them one after the other. They learned to recognize the flavors that go into a successful cup of coffee. Today, coffee traders still judge beans in the same way.

Previous pages: In the mid-1600s, the coffeehouse was where smart gentlemen drank, smoked, and chatted while drinking coffee, known for its ability to promote lively discussion.

The Portuguese government desperately wanted to plant coffee in Brazil, but they had a difficult time getting hold of any living plants. In 1727, a Portuguese official was called in to broker a land dispute between the governors of French and Dutch Guiana. The Portuguese representative resolved the conflict, and at the same time conducted a secret love affair with the wife of the French governor. As he departed for his return trip to Brazil she presented him with a large bouquet of flowers—hidden in the center was a coffee bush ready to be planted. Thus, the Brazilian coffee industry was established.

Coffee soon spread throughout Central and South America. But the growth of the coffee industry had a dark side. When the Dutch introduced coffee to Java, they went into production on a large scale, and they brought in slave labor to work the plantations. Sadly, they established a pattern that followed the commodity as it spread around the world. In the Americas, sugar and tobacco were already grown by

Postcards from a South American coffee plantation in the 1880s show the rigors of the industry.

slaves, and the French, Spanish, and Portuguese saw no reason to do things differently on their American coffee plantations.

Like the other luxury goods that became popular in Europe during the sixteenth, seventeenth, and eighteenth centuries, coffee played a dual role: in Europe, it accelerated the development of both democracy and capitalism, but at the same time it kept those luxuries out of the hands of the people who produced them.

The coffee industry came to depend on slave labor to such an extent that Brazil did not officially abolish slavery until 1888—making it the last country in the Western Hemisphere to do so. And so much of Brazil's arable land was devoted to coffee agriculture that during the 1800s the country had difficulty growing sufficient food crops to feed its citizens. Because all it could export was coffee, Brazil's fortunes (and those of other coffee-producing countries) became completely dependent on the price of coffee in the world market.

CHOOSING COFFEE OVER TEA

The British colonists in North America arrived with a taste for coffee. John Smith, who led the settlers at Jamestown, had traveled in Turkey and was a coffee aficionado. Coffeehouses also crossed the Atlantic with the colonists; in 1689 Boston opened its first coffeehouse.

The English brought coffee to their American colonies, but it was expensive in comparison to tea, which is why the early settlers were tea drinkers. When King George's tax on teas caused the patriots of Boston to stage the Boston Tea Party, the protest was financial and political, but totally unrelated to gastronomy. The history of how people really eat and drink clearly shows that politics plays a small role in our food selection. Price, however, significantly alters the way we eat and drink.

During the Revolutionary War, the American colonists drank coffee because tea was not readily available. When the war was over they

When British settlers in North America protested the tax on tea, the shift toward coffee drinking began.

went right back to drinking tea, which was considerably cheaper.

When the newly formed United States of America went into battle with England for a second time during the War of 1812, the supply of English tea was once again greatly reduced. Americans returned to drinking coffee, but this time the coffee came from Latin America rather than Asia or Africa. It was inexpensive and of the best quality.

After the war, Americans stopped purchasing their tea from the great English tea companies, buying it instead from American shippers. Unfortunately, the knowledge and skills necessary to purchase top-quality tea in the growing areas was not part of the American naval tradition and the quality of the tea coming into the United States declined significantly. It was this reduction in excellence that caused most people to turn to coffee. The choice was very simple: inferior high-priced tea or superior and inexpensive coffee.

African

FOODS IN AMERICA

Many of the foods that have become staples of the American diet came by way of African slaves that were brought to America. Peanuts, bananas, watermelon, rice, yams, and okra all have their roots in Africa and were eaten, cultivated, prepared, and popularized by the early generations of African Americans.

The domestication of plants and animals in Africa goes back at least 6,000 years. One of the basic foods for a number of groups was the yam, and when iron tools were introduced about 2,500 years ago yam production was made easier and crop yields increased rapidly. The people who ate yams developed a higher culture because they had a more reliable source of food than their neighbors. They also developed larger populations. Millions of slaves were taken from West Africa, and the ships that carried them were provisioned with two hundred yams per person.

West Africa and the Atlantic Islands just off the coast of Africa were the staging areas for the European voyages of discovery. On the islands of the Canaries and Madeira, the Spanish and Portuguese tested the plantation system and the use of slaves. When Columbus planted sugar in the Caribbean he also planted the idea of slaves as the labor force—a labor force that came almost exclusively from Africa.

Shrimp and sausage gumbo is part of the "fusion" between African and American cuisines known as Creole cooking.

The process of adapting African foods to the Americas had two distinct stages. The first resulted from the fact that the slaves came from many different tribes with many different gastronomic traditions. When they were brought together on boats and on plantations there was an exchange of food traditions between the different groups.

"You would find people who were rice eaters working side by side with people who were yam eaters, and fish eaters next to meat eaters," explains Jessica B. Harris, a culinary historian and expert on the foods of the African diaspora. "They didn't come from the same place; they didn't speak the same language. They are juxtaposed within this New World and there's a trade off and in the end a new cuisine is created. We call it Creole and it was one of the world's original fusion foods."

In addition to developing native African foods in America, the early generations of African Americans contributed to American cuisine in another way: by substituting readily available American ingredients for the foods of Africa that were no longer at hand. In the process, Africans played a major role in the creation of American cuisine, particularly in the Caribbean and the southern United States.

Crayfish gumbo uses an African-inspired base sauce mixed with a readily available protein.

As Harris explains, "As African cuisine came to the New World, it came with people who were enslaved, and didn't have a choice about what they ate, when they ate, and, in many cases, where they ate it. The only choice they might have had was how they cooked it. A lot of dishes were transformed by the lack of African ingredients and the availability of American ingredients."

"Our mythical Southern cuisine was created by black slave cooks," relates author Karen Hess. "In any house of any importance whatsoever, they had slaves to do the cooking—black hands stirred the pots. It's as simple as that. It produced a phenomenon that the Chinese call 'wok hand' or 'wok signature.' The person who does the cooking influences the dish in extraordinary and mysterious ways. They make the dish their own."

PEANUTS

A peanut is not a nut but a legume, like peas and beans. Unlike peas and beans, however, peanuts are oily, not starchy, and they have an unusual way of growing. As soon as the plant starts to germinate it grows backward down into the ground where the peanuts mature in their pods.

Peanuts are native to South America and have been a staple crop in Bolivia, Peru, and Brazil for almost four thousand years. Archaeologists report that ancient Peruvians ate peanuts as a snack food, and their city streets were littered with peanut shells, not unlike the stands at a modern baseball park.

By the early 1500s, the Portuguese sailing along the coast of Brazil became aware of the peanut's value and began taking it on their ships. Peanuts keep for months and can be eaten raw, which makes them ideal for sea voyages.

In addition to sailing along the east coast of Brazil, the Portuguese were also sailing down the west coast of Africa. Their objective on both sides of the Atlantic was the same—

Portuguese sailors took the South American peanut to Africa where it was quickly adopted into African cuisine.

they wanted to develop trade routes to the Far East. It was on these routes that they brought peanuts to West Africa. By 1510, the peanut was a staple at Portuguese trading posts.

Prior to the arrival of the Portuguese, the people of West Africa ate Bambara nuts which are similar to peanuts. So when peanuts arrived they were quickly accepted. The Africans soon discovered that the peanut produced a higher yield, provided more oil, and was easier to grow than the Bambara. It pushed out the Bambara and became a staple crop across West Africa. In fact, the peanut became so closely associated with Africa that even leading botanists did not realize they originated in South America until the mid-1800s.

Peanuts arrived in North America via the slave trade. By the early 1700s, Portuguese slave traders put them on board the slave ships that went from Africa to the Caribbean.

"Most people thought that the peanut was an African food that came to the Western Hemisphere with African slaves," explains Harris. "But it really was a South American food that jumped over Central America and

Mexico by going to Africa and then back to North America. And when it came back to the Americas it came back with its African name."

In the Bantu language the Bambara nut was called a *goober* Africans used this word to describe the peanut, and when the Africans traveled across the Atlantic they took the old name and the new food with them. They also took the ways they had developed for using the peanut. They ate them raw, or roasted, or boiled—they prepared them in soups and stews and used peanut oil for frying.

On plantations where slaves were allowed to grow their own foods, peanuts were always part of the crop. A few white planters, including Thomas Jefferson, attempted to grow peanuts as a cash crop, but most whites used them for hog feed. But Africans were doing the cooking in many white households and they slowly introduced peanuts into the cuisine of the South.

In 1791, a slave rebellion in Haiti sent hundreds of French planters and their house-hold slaves to Philadelphia. The household servants brought a taste for peanuts with them and peanut recipes soon appeared in early American cookbooks. By the early 1800s, African women were working as

peanut vendors. They sold peanuts and peanut cakes in the markets of Philadelphia. In the years before packaged snack foods, peanuts were a favorite snack of the working classes.

Theatergoers munched on peanuts and littered the floors with the shells. Critics began to complain about the peanut-eating audience in the cheap seats, and the notion of the "peanut gallery" was born.

Agricultural inventor George Washington Carver promoted the peanut and came up with countless uses for the legume. Born in Missouri in 1864, Carver was raised by white farmers. It is said that the infant Carver and his mother were kidnapped for ransom by slave raiders from Arkansas and that Moses Carver, the farmer who became his adoptive father, gave a three-hundred dollar horse to his rescuers—a fitting beginning for a legendary character.

Carver was an excellent student and eventually got a master's degree in agriculture, becoming the first black faculty member at the agricultural college that eventually

Although it originated in South America, the peanut has long been a staple in Africa, where it all but replaced the similar native bambara nut. The peanut has been used in many dishes, including peanut soup, peanut bread, and peanut brittle.

became Iowa State University. In 1896 Booker T. Washington invited Carver to head Tuskegee Institute's new Department of Agriculture. He took the job and worked there for almost five decades.

For years, Carver had been searching for a replacement crop for cotton farmers who had lost their livelihoods to boll weevil infestations. Ideally, the crop would be one they could eat themselves if market prices dropped. His search led him to the peanut.

In 1916 he published a pamphlet, entitled *How to Grow the Peanut and 105 Ways of Preparing It for Human Consumption*, which set the tone for the rest of his career. Carver became a tireless advocate of peanut cultivation and consumption, and he turned his imagination to finding new uses for the peanut.

Carver served dinners consisting entirely of peanut products: peanut soup, peanut-based meat substitutes, peanut beverages, and peanut desserts. By the end of

George Washington Carver (left) was an eloquent proponent of the peanut. Although he found myriad uses for the peanut, he did not invent peanut butter, above left.

his career, he had developed over three hundred peanut products, including such unlikely items as wallboard, creams, paints, soaps, and dyes.

Carver was a riveting public speaker and in 1921 testified before Congress in favor of a tariff protecting domestic peanut farmers. He made a historic presentation during which he showed an incredulous Ways and Means Committee an assortment of peanut items, including candies, ice creams, cakes, breakfast cereals, and breads, as well as animal feeds and wood stains. He never left the lecture circuit, and spoke widely on the virtues of the peanut for the rest of his career.

However, he did not invent peanut butter—and neither did John Harvey Kellogg, who did coin the term "peanut butter" when he introduced it as a health food in 1894. Africans had been using nut pastes made with a mortar and pestle even before encountering the peanut itself. A thousand years ago, the Aztecs made a peanut paste, very similar to peanut butter. Curiously, the Aztecs used their peanut paste not as a food but as a toothpaste.

BANANAS

The banana was first cultivated around three thousand years ago in Malaysia, and eventually became a staple food throughout Southeast Asia. Malaysian sailors spread the fruit throughout the islands of the Pacific, where bananas, along with their starchier cousins, plantains (the plants differ only in that the plantain's fruit contains less moisture), became primary crops in Polynesia and the Philippines.

By the sixth century B.C. bananas grew widely in India, where Alexander the Great encountered them during his Indian campaign of 327 B.C. The Roman historian Pliny referred to the banana as the "fruit of the sages" based on Alexander's reports of Indian intellectuals using banana trees to shade themselves from the sun.

The Arab traders who made their way to Malaysia in the 1600s were the first to introduce the banana to Africa. Early on, the banana became part of Islamic legend.

A Honduran woman hides behind the giant leaf of a banana tree.

Koranic scholars identified the banana—not the apple—as the forbidden fruit in Paradise. According to their interpretation, Europeans, in their translations of Genesis, may have confused the banana with the Middle Eastern fig—and if Adam and Eve were looking for something to cover their nakedness, a huge banana leaf makes more sense as a loincloth than a fig leaf.

Bananas spread quickly across the African continent and became an important food crop. The fruit picked up the name by which we know it today in West Africa, on the Guinea coast. The name stuck, since this was where modern Europeans had their first significant contact with the fruit.

The banana plant, though it can reach heights of thirty feet, is not really a tree but a gigantic herb,

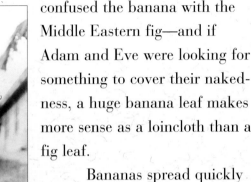

related to the lily and the orchid. The "trunk" of the banana plant is no more than a bunch of tightly rolled leaves. It is a tropical plant and refuses to bear significant quantities of fruit north of thirty degrees latitude. So even though Europeans had been running into the banana for a couple thousand years, it was not until the 1400s—when Portuguese traders met West African banana planters— that they accepted it as an important food.

In 1482, the Portuguese brought bananas to their sugar plantations on the Atlantic island of Madeira. Spanish traders soon imported the banana to the Canary Islands. As the European powers moved their plantations to the Americas, bananas followed. Portuguese slave ships were provisioned with bananas when they left Africa, and by 1516 the Spanish were growing bananas in the Caribbean as food for the expanding population of African slaves. The banana quickly adapted to the American tropics, and became a basic food in Central and South America.

Bananas, imported from Central America, were introduced in the United States in 1876.

In the 1870s and 1880s, a group of U.S. fruit merchants began importing bananas from Panama, Costa Rica, and Jamaica. Bananas were introduced to the North American public at the 1876 Centennial Exposition in Philadelphia and soon became popular in the United States. At first they were a luxury item, but as shipping methods and refrigeration improved and prices dropped, bananas became equally popular with the working classes.

The fruit merchants who introduced the banana to the American public joined together and became the United Fruit Company. During the first half of the twentieth century, United Fruit exercised tremendous influence over the nations of Central and South America.

United Fruit's marketing campaigns made breakfast cereals incomplete without bananas and did much to make Americans and Europeans into banana consumers. The banana economy entered the popular imagination through songs, like Harry Belafonte's 1950s hit "Day-O (The Banana Boat Song)," an idyllic calypso work song sung from the perspective of dockworkers loading bananas.

Green bananas on the "tree" are commonly thought of as a fruit. However, the banana is technically an herb—a plant or plant part valued for its medicinal, savory, or aromatic qualities.

RICE

According to some estimates, half the world's population depends on rice. It is thought to have originated in India and has been grown in China for some three thousand years; cultures all over Asia began growing rice soon after it reached China.

"When Americans think about rice they associate it with China, but the fact is that the cultivation of rice in America was something that was learned from Africans," explains Hess. "African methods, African know-how, African cooking techniques, and at the beginning, even African rice."

In West Africa, a native rice species, *Oryza glaberrina*, was domesticated independently of the Asian varieties and has been cultivated there since 1500 B.C.—hundreds of years before its Asian cousins were grown in China. In the tidal lowlands of the Senegal and Gambia rivers, an area that became known as the "Grain Coast" or "Rice Coast," African farmers developed a system of wetlands for rice cultivation that resembles the paddy system used in Asia. On the Rice Coast, men did the heavy work of building the irrigation systems, but women were

African women work the rice fields transplanting and harvesting rice in an irrigated system similar to the paddies of Asia.

responsible for planting and cultivating the rice that they cooked.

Europeans in the Americas began rice growing on dry land irrigated only by rainfall. At first it was food for the growing slave population, but it became an export commodity by the beginning of the 1700s. South Carolina emerged as the center of rice production in North America. As rice gained economic importance, a plantation system for its production developed.

The plantation owners in the South Carolina low country were well aware of the traditions of African rice growing, and the rice economy that developed in the American South depended on African slave labor.

"The land from southern Senegal to Liberia is rice country," explains Harris. "There is an indigenous African rice, that is a wet rice. It is grown in water, according to a certain system. The Carolina planters knew that, and paid a top price for slaves from that part of Africa who understood rice cultivation.

Previous pages: African curried fish on rice is an exotic and spicy main dish that is served using the whole fish.

And those folks built the rice industry in Carolina. The entire rice system of Carolina is based on an African task system."

Traders seem to have sought out slaves—especially those from Senegal and Gambia—who would bring rice-growing expertise. These Africans introduced the flood-control techniques they had used in West Africa and built an elaborate irrigation system that made the Carolina rice industry possible.

In the process they made "Carolina Rice" a prized export to Europe—and at the same time made South Carolina planters some of the richest people in North America. Europeans were so enamored of Carolina rice that when the British took Charleston during the Revolutionary War, they removed the entire rice crop and shipped it home to England.

African rice cooking has left its mark on all the cuisines of the Americas. The familiar American dishes of rice and beans—Hoppin' John in the southern United States, Jamaican and Haitian rice and peas, Cuba's *Moros y Cristianos,* and the rice-and-beans dishes found all over Latin America—are all of African origin.

Africans, who had been cultivating rice for centuries, brought their flood-irrigation technique to America where their expertise helped spawn a rice industry in the United States.

YAMS

Yams are native to both Southeast Asia and West Africa, and have been growing in both areas for about eight thousand years. Starchy porridges made from grains or tubers and eaten with a sauce or meat are common all over Africa; *fufu* is the West African variety, typically made with yams that have been boiled and then ground to a paste with a mortar and pestle.

In the early 1500s, the Portuguese brought the sweet potato to Africa, where, like the peanut, it was quickly accepted because it was so similar to an existing crop. While the peanut largely replaced the Bambara groundnut, the sweet potato was added to African menus, grown and used alongside, rather than in place of, the yam.

True African yams made their way to the Americas with the slaves themselves.

While yams—which are best grown in the tropics— were never cultivated in any quantity in North America, they did take root in the Caribbean and in South America. In Latin America yams are still grown and eaten, prepared mashed or fried in recipes that draw on thousands of years of use in Africa and the Americas.

North Americans have been confusing yams and sweet potatoes for several hundred years, perhaps because African Americans described the sweet potato using the same word they had used at home for the yam. Today, the sweeter, smoother-fleshed varieties of sweet potato are commonly referred to as yams, although true yams are actually even sweeter than sweet potatoes. The confusion is perpetuated by the fact that several varieties of sweet potatoes are even marketed as yams. Yams, which have a skin resembling bark and white flesh, rather than the orange flesh and smoother skin of the sweet potato, are still rarely encountered in the United States.

What are commonly thought of as yams are actually sweet potatoes— long, orange tubers with a smooth potato-like skin. True yams are only grown in Africa and have white flesh and a woody skin. Yams are actually sweeter than the sweet potato.

OKRA

"Okra dishes are perhaps the most typically African of all of the dishes commonly served in the United States," relates Hess. "While today okra is closely associated with the idea of Southern cuisine, and with the Creole culture of Louisiana in particular, okra was brought to the Americas as food for slaves, and the okra dishes of the Americas make some of the clearest culinary connections to Africa."

Okra, a relative of cotton and hibiscus, is native to Africa, probably originating either in the rainforests of western Sudan, or in the Nile Valley, around what is now Ethiopia.

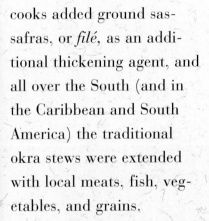

As it spread north and west, okra became a fixture in many African cuisines. Okra pods are filled with a mucilaginous sap that is essential for the creation of the gummy, slippery texture that is a hallmark of African soups and stews.

Okra came to the Americas with the slave trade, and was grown widely in Central and South America. While it was never a plantation crop, it was an important subsistence crop—wherever Africans were permitted to grow food for their own use, they planted okra. And they took the okra recipes they knew in Africa and revised them for use in the Americas, establishing what Jessica Harris calls a "gumbo trail" that reaches back to West Africa.

Okra has become almost a cuisine unto itself—it is the primary ingredient of gumbo, one of the dishes most closely associated with the Creole culture of New Orleans. In fact, the name "gumbo" is derived from the Angolan name for okra in the Twi language of Ghana. In Louisiana, cooks added ground sassafras, or *filé*, as an additional thickening agent, and all over the South (and in the Caribbean and South America) the traditional okra stews were extended with local meats, fish, vegetables, and grains.

"When you start to talk about the influence of black cooks on the foods of this hemisphere, you almost don't know where to start," comments Harris. "The soupy stews over starches, gumbos, leafy greens . . . all of those things are African . . . and the whole technique of frying in deep oil is arguably African."

The African influence on American cooking has been wide-ranging—from the rice and beans dishes of Latin America to the fried chicken and gumbos of the American South, from rice pilafs and peanut butter to watermelons and sweet potato pie, American food has been shaped by the contributions of African foods and African American cooks.

Okra, a common ingredient in African dishes, grows in fuzzy green pods that contain a sticky juice used as a thickener in gumbo dishes. Okra is also eaten boiled, steamed, baked, grilled, and stir-fried.

❋

THE STORY OF
Chocolate

In the spring of 1502, Columbus set sail on his fourth and final voyage. His objective was to reach Asia. He believed that the islands of the West Indies, which he had reached on earlier expeditions, were just offshore China and Japan.

Columbus's first landfall was in the Bay Islands about thirty miles north of Honduras. As his ship sat at anchor, the crew saw a tremendous dugout canoe. Columbus's son Ferdinand reported that the canoe, which was roughly as long as a Venetian galley, had amidships a shelter fashioned of palm leaves. Under this were the children, the women, and the cargo, which included almond-like beans.

Ferdinand wrote in 1502: "They seemed to hold these almonds at a great price; for when they were brought on board ship together with their goods, I observed that when any of these almonds fell, they all stooped to pick them up, as if an eye had fallen." It was a Mayan trading canoe, about 150 feet long and carrying a cargo of cacao beans. Columbus was the first European to come in contact with the source of chocolate.

The Maya dominated the east coast of Central America from 250 to 900 A.D. Their culture, art, and architecture were on a level with that of ancient Greece and Renaissance Italy. And they were great chocolate masters.

Chocolate is called the "food of the gods." There is a chocolate for almost any taste, ranging from light to dark, from sweet to bitter.

The Maya had a written language and often wrote about chocolate. In an ancient Mayan book called the Dresden Codex, which predates the arrival of the Spanish, there are pictures of seated gods holding cacao pods and dishes filled with cacao beans. The commentary explains that cacao is to be offered during New Year celebrations. Cacao pods also appear on carved vessels that were placed in the graves of important members of Mayan society.

Chocolate drinks played an important part in Mayan gatherings and celebrations. Women poured chocolate from one jar to another, creating a foam that was the most desirable part of the beverage. An illustration on an eighth-century vase from northern Guatemala shows a Mayan king seated on his throne with a vase for chocolate drinks.

According to Professor Emeritus in Anthropology at Yale University Michael D. Coe, an expert on Mayan civilization, "The

For centuries before its discovery by Columbus, Mayan society had been drinking chocolate at gatherings and celebrations such as those held at this Mayan temple in the Yucatan.

Maya used chocolate to seal pacts, or to cement marriage relationships. . . . It was used during negotiations of all sorts among the Maya. And, in fact, because it was used as money at the same time as it was used as a drink, it had the cachet that champagne holds today."

The Aztecs picked up the use of chocolate and cacao from the Maya. They worshiped Quetzalcoatl, the god who gave chocolate to the world.

"The Aztecs had the same approach to chocolate as the Mayas," explains Coe. "It wasn't a drink for ordinary people. It was a drink for the elite . . . as it became later on in Europe for the top echelons of society. And this included the nobility, the king and his retinue, the palace, and the great warriors. . . . Chocolate had almost a sanctified aspect to it. In fact, it was conceived symbolically as human blood. And so it was really like Communion wine in many respects."

CHOCOLATE AND THE CHURCH

When chocolate reached Europe, it first became accepted as a health drink. But there was one more barrier it had to pass in order to be fully accepted, and that was ecclesiastical. The main problem was that the Catholic Church could not decide whether chocolate was a medicine, which could be taken at any time, or a food, which would not be allowed during periods of fasting.

The Society of Jesus, the official name of the Jesuits, was founded in 1534 and was the militant arm of the church—zealous defenders of the pope's supremacy. They maintained a tightly controlled worldwide organization. In 1650, Jesuit leaders prohibited Jesuits from drinking chocolate, but quickly rescinded the decision when students started leaving the seminary.

"Once it had been decided by the ecclesiastical authorities that chocolate did not break the fast—in other words, that during Lent you could take chocolate because it was not considered a food—the Jesuits went into high gear and started a commercial operation," explains anthropologist Michael D. Coe. "They grew cacao commercially through much of Latin America. They drank a lot of it themselves, too; they were big chocolate imbibers. But they definitely shipped a lot of chocolate back and made a lot of money."

In a report dated 1639, a Jesuit describes what he saw along the Amazon River:

"The banks are so full of . . . those trees which produce the fruit so esteemed in New Spain and everywhere else where they know what Chocolate is; which cultivated is so profitable that every tree, yearly and free from all expenses, gives a profit of 8 silver reales, and one can easily see how little work it takes to cultivate these trees on this river, as without any application of art, nature fills them with abundant fruit."

Religious orders were allowed to ship goods without paying duties, which made the Jesuit cacao crop quite lucrative.

Saint Ignatius of Loyola, shown above, was a Spanish prelate and founder of the Society of Jesus, which was dedicated to the education of young men in religious teachings. For a time, the Jesuits were commanded to withhold drinking chocolate on fast days, a command that led to an exodus from the order.

The Aztecs flavored the chocolate drink with allspice, vanilla, honey, chilies, corn, and flowers, but the drink was unpleasing to the Spaniards who sampled it.

"When the Spaniards first came to Mexico, they saw people drinking chocolate and were offered it and tried it," explains Coe. "They thought it was horrible. In fact, one of our sources, an Italian traveler and historian, says it was only fit for pigs. It was so bad. It was bitter. They didn't like the color of it. It made your mouth black. Or if they mixed it with a spice called achiote, which is red, it made your mouth look red and dyed your lips. . . . They thought it was the most disgusting stuff. It wasn't until later that they realized how good it was."

The production of cacao was the most important business of the period, and among the Mesoamericans, the beans themselves became a form of currency. The first person to call America the "New World" was Pietro Martire d'Anghiera, an Italian living in Spain who in 1516 wrote a book about the events taking place in Mexico and the Caribbean. The book was called *De Orbe Novo*, "The New World," and in it he reported on the use of cacao beans as currency:

"They have money which I call happy because in acquiring it they do not pull the earth apart as we do in search of gold and silver because their happy money grows on trees."

The Spanish adopted cacao beans as currency to trade with Mayans in the Americas. When the beans traveled back to Spain, they were valued for their medicinal purposes.

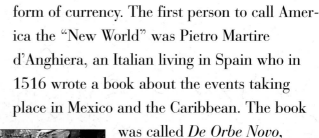

Cacao trees produce the beans used to create a bitter chocolate drink favored by the natives of the Americas.

Spanish Conquistador Hernando Cortez used cacao beans as currency to trade with the Native Americans. The Spanish did not appreciate the bitter taste of the Aztec drink, and only began using it at home when mixed with sugar to make it sweet.

CHOCOLATE AS MEDICINE

The Spanish decided chocolate was not only good, but good for you. European medical theories of the fifteenth and sixteenth centuries were primitive. The Native Americans had an advanced system based on their extensive knowledge of plants and how to use them to effect real cures. When word of the Americas' pharmacy reached King Philip II of Spain, he sent his Royal Physician Francisco Hérnandez to Mexico. And even though cacao was not used by Native Americans as a medicine, Hérnandez included it in his bag of cures.

Dried cacao beans are ground into a powder. While native Mexicans never used cacao for medicinal purposes, the Spanish thought it would cure fevers and intestinal pains.

Hérnandez informed the king that the cacao seed was not simply nourishing, but had been found to cure fevers in hot weather. And when pepper is added, it "warms the stomach and perfumes the breath . . . combats poisons, [and] alleviates intestinal pains and colics." However, Hérnandez warned the king, it could also "excite the venereal appetite."

In seventeenth-century France, in the baroque palaces of the rich and powerful, chocolate began its conquest of Europe. Chocolate traveled from one royal court to another as a medicine. But it soon became appreciated for its taste and stimulating effect on the nervous system. Chocolate contains theobromine, which is an alkaloid, and like all alkaloids it will stimulate the central nervous system. It also contains small amounts of caffeine, but how the caffeine will affect you is a function of your individual tolerance as well as your cultural beliefs. If you think a cup of chocolate will wake you up, it probably will. If you were brought up to believe it has a soothing effect, relaxation will probably be your response.

During the mid-1600s, Dr. Henry Stubbes was the great English authority on chocolate and personally prepared it for King Charles II. Stubbes, like most of his contemporaries in England and on the Continent, considered chocolate an aphrodisiac. He published an essay on the erotic properties of chocolate, which sent chocolate sales through the roof.

The cacao bean finally made its debut and was presented to European royalty in 1544. The Dominican Friars who were among the first and most energetic missionaries in the Americas, took a delegation of Mayan nobles to visit Prince Philip in Spain. Among the gifts they brought were bowls of chocolate. But it would be forty years before regular shipments started arriving.

In 1660, Maria Teresa, daughter of the king of Spain, married Louis XIV, king of France. The new queen loved chocolate. But the king did not and so she sipped her chocolate in private. Within ten years, in spite of Louis's opinion, drinking chocolate became popular with the French upper class. Louis XIV granted a royal monopoly for chocolate. In France, chocolate was tightly controlled by a centralized authority and was only available to the aristocracy.

King Louis XIV married the daughter of King Philip IV of Spain. The new queen brought her love of chocolate with her to England.

SERVING CHOCOLATE

The Spanish nobles originally drank chocolate from small open bowls that they got from the Aztecs. One day at court in Lima, the viceroy of Peru was horrified to see a lady spill a bowl of chocolate on her dress. He commissioned a silversmith to make a saucer with a collar-like ring in the center. The chocolate cup fits into the ring, which holds it safely in place. The invention was called a *mancerina* after the viceroy, who was the Marques de Mancera. Exported back to Europe, it became the most popular service for liquid chocolate.

In pre-Spanish times, the Mesoamericans poured the chocolate liquid from one jar to another in order to produce the desired foam— a time consuming process. The Spanish colonists introduced the *molinillo* in the sixteenth century—a wooden utensil that they placed into a pot and twirled between their hands. The French covered the pot with a wooden lid and made a hole in the top for the molinillo. They called it a *chocolatière* and it quickly became the preferred way of making the foam.

Where chocolate has been a popular drink, different serving bowls and utensils have been designed to achieve the drink's desired froth.

In 1655, English forces took the island of Jamaica from the Spanish. Cacao plantations were big business on Jamaica, and England quickly realized cacao's gastronomic and commercial value. Jamaica became Great Britain's major source of cacao. Four years after Jamaica was taken, an article ran in an English newspaper:

"Chocolate, an excellent West India drink, sold in Queen's-Head-alley, in Bishopsgate-street, by a Frenchman . . . being the first man who did sell it in England. There you may have it ready to drink and also unmade at easy rates, and taught the use thereof, it being for its excellent qualities so much esteemed in all places. It cures and preserves the body of many diseases."

Chocolate, coffee, tea, and sugar all entered England at the same time and at the highest social levels, but that soon changed. Unlike France, England was a nation of shopkeepers. And when chocolate came into the country anybody who could afford to buy a cup of chocolate could have it. The rising middle class began to drink chocolate in coffeehouses that were hotbeds of political debate. The first English parliamentary parties used to meet in these coffeehouses.

Chocolate, as a hot beverage, quickly became popular in coffeehouses, along with tea and coffee.

When colonial officials were assigned to their posts in Virginia and Massachusetts, they brought chocolate to North America. But in Europe, it remained the drink of the upper class.

Since the end of the 1800s, Switzerland has dominated the world of chocolate. Today its citizens are the number-one consumers, averaging almost twelve pounds of chocolate per person, per year.

In addition to creating exquisite chocolate confections, the Swiss raised cows that gave them some of the world's finest milk. In 1879, Henri Nestlé, the Swiss chemist who developed powdered milk, combined forces with Daniel Peter, a Swiss chocolate maker, to produce the world's first milk chocolate. During the same year, another Swiss, Rudolphe Lindt, invented the "conching" process. It reduces the size of the particles and gives solid chocolate a smooth mellowness.

The founder of modern botany gave the cacao tree a Latin name that translates as "food of the gods"—which seems quite appropriate as many consider chocolate to be heavenly.

Not surprisingly, it was a Swiss duo that invented the world's first milk chocolate. Daniel Peter's attempt to invent a creamy chocolate was perfected when he partnered with Henri Nestle, who had developed powdered milk.

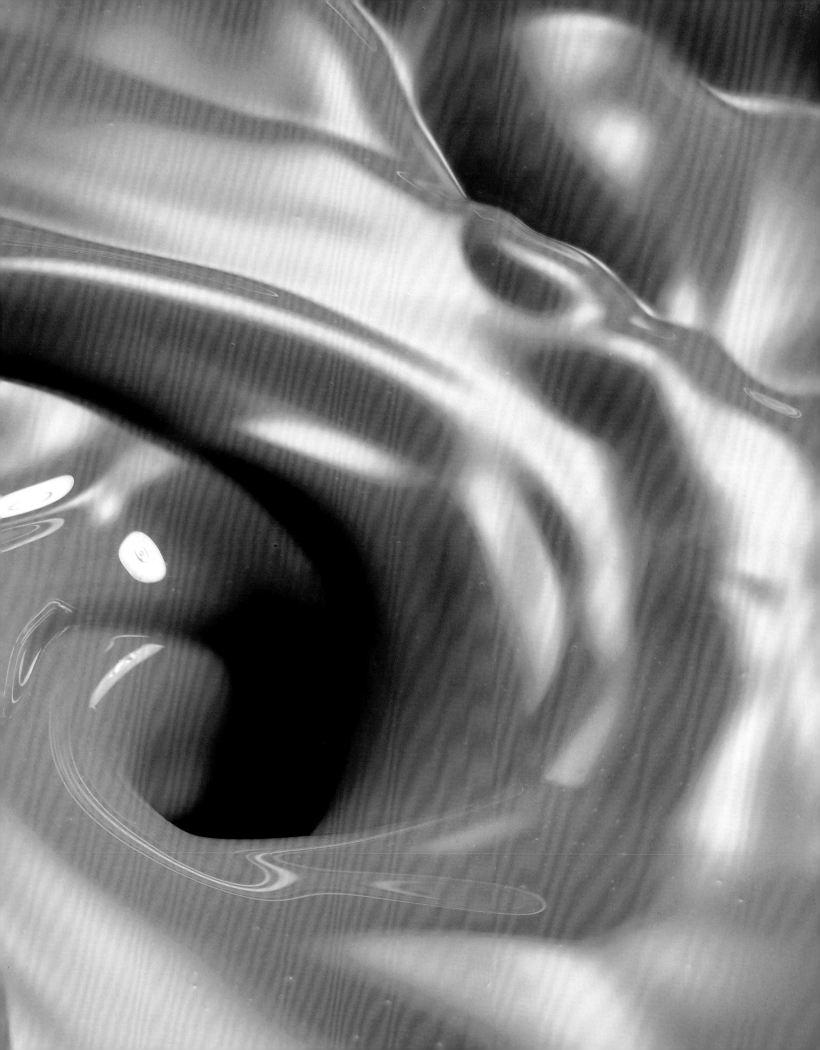

FROM THE BEAN TO THE BAR

Chocolate comes from the cacao tree, which is difficult to grow, uncooperative, and moody. It refuses to bear fruit unless it is growing inside a narrow strip of land near the equator. It demands moisture throughout the year, and the temperature must never fall below sixty degrees Fahrenheit.

The cacao tree is one of the world's most inefficient biological systems. Each tree will produce hundreds of flowers, but only one to three percent of them will bear fruit—and the tree will take about three years to get around to that. The small flowers are pollinated exclusively by midges, little bugs that live on the forest floor.

After four or five months, each successfully pollinated

Cacao flowers spring from the trunk of the tree and from them the cacao pods are produced. A half-opened cacao pod reveals the seeds contained inside.

flower will produce a large pod containing thirty to forty almond-shaped seeds or beans surrounded by a sweet pulp. The pods grow directly on the trunk.

The plant cannot open the pod itself—it depends on squirrels and small monkeys to disperse its seeds. The monkeys and squirrels steal the pods for the pulp, but discard the bitter beans.

Workers split the pods to get to the seeds and surrounding pulp. The two are allowed to sit and ferment together for five or six days. The pulp becomes liquid and drains away. The seeds germinate briefly and develop their chocolate taste. They are dried and shipped to

the chocolate factory where they are roasted and shelled.

The remaining "nibs" are ground in a machine that works like a giant food processor. The liquid that comes out is called "cocoa liquor." The cocoa liquor goes into a cylinder where it is put under enormous pressure, and the liquid cocoa butter is separated from the solids, which are called cocoa.

In 1823, Coenraad Van Houten, a Dutch chemist, invented a process called "Dutching," which removes most of the fat from the chocolate solids. Van Houten placed the chocolate liquor, which contains fifty-three percent fat, into a hydraulic press that pressed out the cocoa butter. What was left was a disc of chocolate with a fat content of twenty-seven to twenty-eight percent. He pulverized this disc to produce a fine powder, which we now know as cocoa.

The age-old thick and foamy drink was replaced by the easily prepared, more digestible cocoa. With Van Houten's invention, manufacturers could make inexpensive chocolate for the masses. The cocoa butter that was separated out is also a valuable product. It is used in the making of top-quality chocolate and in the manufacture of cosmetics and pharmaceuticals.

In 1847, an Englishman blended together cocoa powder, sugar, and melted cocoa butter to produce a paste that was poured into a mold—the world's first chocolate bar.

Today there are countless varieties of chocolate bar mixed with ingredients such as nuts, caramel, marshmallow, and puffed rice, to name of few.

THE STORY OF
Sugar

People have a built-in love of sweetness. Some researchers believe that our attraction to sweet foods goes back millions of years, to a time when most foods in nature that were good to eat were sweet and most foods that were bitter were poisonous. The people who loved sweetness were more likely to multiply, those who didn't, were not.

Twelve thousand years ago in New Guinea, people started chewing on sugar cane to satisfy their sweet tooth. About ten thousand years later, in India, people learned to make solid sugar from the cane juice—a skill that traders eventually brought to the Middle East.

Starting in the seventh century A.D., Arab armies began marching out of the Middle East, conquering North Africa and parts of southern Europe. They invaded Spain and introduced sugar to the Spanish, who slowly adopted it. Six hundred years later, only a few Europeans could afford it.

But during the eleventh and twelfth centuries, things began to change. The Christian knights who went to the Middle East during the Crusades came in contact with sugar—a basic part of Middle Eastern medicine and gastronomy. The knights loved it. When they returned to Europe they spread the word.

Sugar comes cubed, powdered, granulated, light brown, dark brown, and crystal white. The human craving for sugar is believed to be a product of evolution.

JUST A SPOONFUL OF SUGAR

Throughout its extraordinary history, sugar has been used as a medicine. More than two thousand years ago, a Greek visitor to India reported that he had found a hard honey, called *saccharon,* with a consistency like salt. It was dissolved in water and drunk as a medicine for the stomach.

From the tenth to the eighteenth century sugar was considered a wonder drug and prescribed for coughs, sore throats, labored breathing, and stomach ailments. Every medicine used during the Black Plague contained sugar. To cure impaired vision, doctors blew powdered sugar into the eye.

Sugar had become so much a part of medicine that people used the expression "like an apothecary without sugar" to describe a state of total helplessness or desperation.

Albert van Aachen, a monk who recorded stories of the First Crusade, wrote in 1096, "In the fields of the plains of Tripoli can be found in abundance a honey reed which they call *Zuchra;* the people are accustomed to suck enthusiastically on these reeds, delighting themselves with their beneficial juices, and seem unable to sate themselves with this pleasure in spite of their sweetness. . . . It was on this sweet-tasting sugar cane that people sustained themselves during the sieges . . . when they were tormented by fearsome hunger."

But the Crusaders did more than just introduce Europe to the idea of sugar. During the early years of the Crusades, Europeans conquered large parts of the Middle East; in one area, called the kingdom of Jerusalem, they oversaw the cultivation of sugar cane and the production of sugar. The mills are still visible at a site near Jericho.

The Knights of Malta got into the sugar trade and so did the merchants of Venice. As a result of the Crusades, Europeans turned sugar production and distribution into a small but highly profitable business.

In wealthy households, sugar was used in tiny amounts with other spices to smooth out flavors or to soften an acidic taste, not to sweeten foods so much as make their taste more agreeable. Cooks learned to make a simple syrup from sugar and water and immerse fruits in the syrup to preserve them.

The first Crusaders observed the Middle Eastern peoples' use of sugar and brought their knowledge back to England.

SUGAR ON DISPLAY

One result of sugar's ability to combine with other ingredients was the introduction of marzipan paste, an edible blend of sugar and almonds that could be used to form sculptures.

During the 1200s, bakers in France and England started making sugar sculptures for royal dinners. These were called "subtleties"—artistic forms created as objects of beauty that were to be admired, then eaten. Persians had long molded sugar into edible art. There is a remarkable account that describes a life-size mosque in Egypt built entirely of sugar for a celebration: At the close of the festivities, beggars were invited to eat the building.

Because of the large quantities of sugar required and its expense, in Christian Europe subtleties only decorated the tables of the nobles and leaders of the church. During the fifteenth and sixteenth centuries, subtleties were all the rage. In Italy, costly and precise replicas of the works of great sculptors like Bernini and Michelangelo were shaped by bakers who were considered artists in their own right.

The idea of using sugar to embody feelings was so powerful that subtleties have survived into modern times. Decorated wedding cakes, birthday cakes, and anniversary cakes commemorate important events and mark their significance. Even the yellow marshmallow chicks sold at Easter are modern subtleties.

Marzipan is a confection of almond paste, sugar, and egg whites that is shaped into various forms, including these animal- and fruit-shaped treats.

During the thirteenth and fourteenth centuries, the use of sugar in Europe was increasing, and by the early fifteenth century the governments of Spain and Portugal were encouraging entrepreneurs to set up sugar plantations on the Atlantic islands off the coast of Africa—Portugal took Madeira, Spain took the Canaries.

On Madeira, the Portuguese wanted to produce something that would be in great demand in the cities of Europe—something they could produce cheaper, better, faster, and in greater quantity than anyone else. Honeybees were producing honey and wax for export. Wheat and wine were doing well, but nobody was getting rich. They needed something that would bring in the big bucks, and that turned out to be sugar.

The colonists devoted themselves to the production of sugar, and by the end of the 1400s, they were exporting almost four million pounds of sugar to London, Paris, Rome, and Constantinople.

Christopher Columbus was well aware that sugar was a highly profitable crop. His mother-in-law owned a sugar plantation on the island of Madeira, and Columbus had earned some money transporting sugar from there to the Italian port city of Genoa. During his second voyage to the New World, he planted sugar cane in what is now the Dominican Republic. It was the first sugar cane planted in the Americas.

Sugar cane was cultivated and processed on plantations in the Americas as well as those on the islands off the coast of Africa.

The Caribbean islands were perfectly suited for the production of sugar cane. They had lots of flat land, plenty of water, and a climate that was hot enough but not too dry. By 1640, sugar cane had become the crop of choice in Haiti, Puerto Rico, Jamaica, and Cuba.

The Spanish dominated the Caribbean throughout the 1500s, but the 1600s belonged to the English. They fought the most, conquered the most colonies, imported the most slaves, and moved faster and further than anyone else. They were the primary designers of the plantation system that was used to produce tobacco, rice, and cotton; but the most important product by far was sugar. And England's consumption of sugar kept pace with the new supply.

The natural molasses in raw sugar gives it a light amber color and a sweet, rich taste. Following pages: Assorted white and brown sugars make a beautiful display.

SUGAR CANE PRODUCTION

The production of sugar is a difficult process. It starts with the cultivation of the cane—a tall grass with sweet, juicy stalks that grow to a thickness of two inches and a height of twelve to fifteen feet. It takes nine to eighteen months to ripen. As a rule, sugar cane produces more calories per unit of land in a given time than any other crop in its climate.

7002.   Cutting Sugar Cane.

Cane looks like bamboo, but instead of having a hollow center, it is filled with a sappy pulp. The cane must be cut as soon as it is ripe or it begins to lose some of the sucrose in the juice. And as soon as it is cut, the juice must be extracted or it will ferment and rot.

7005.   Loading Sugar Cane in Field, Cuba.

The sugar cane industry has historically required tight schedules to ensure the cane is processed immediately after it is cut, before the juice ferments.

The cane is taken to the plantation's milling operations where it is chopped, pressed, and pounded to extract the juice. Through a series of complicated heating and cooling processes, the sucrose crystals are formed from the juice.

Workers on tight schedules are needed to coordinate the field activities with operations in the mill. The labor needed to quickly carry out the work is a serious economic challenge for sugar makers.

"The plantation necessarily involved two kinds of labor force. Unskilled, to do the cutting and hard labor," explains Johns Hopkins Professor Emeritus of anthropology Sidney W. Mintz, "and skilled, to do the quasi-chemical processes involved in manufacturing the sugar. Because it takes this particular form, it's an enterprise in which time matters. So we have an enterprise very early in human history that involves two kinds of labor force: factory and field. And an element of time discipline. This made these enterprises really quite exceptional in the history of industry. You've got some of the main features of modern capitalist enterprise, but the real sticking point here is that the labor force, for New World plantations at least, was almost entirely enslaved. And this was true almost from their very beginnings until the middle of the nineteenth century."

African slaves brought to work in the fields provided a continual supply of free labor. During four hundred years of African slavery, at least ten million people were shipped to the Americas.

Sugar production in the Caribbean became a key to England's economic development. To process the sugar cane, English plantation owners built mills and then factories to make the milling machinery. They needed to feed and clothe the slave population, so a salt-cod business developed, and then a textile industry.

The English built ships to transport goods to and from its islands. To coordinate all these activities, they developed international trading companies that gave England worldwide economic leverage.

Trading companies moved goods—and people—across the Atlantic Ocean in a pattern known as the "triangular trade." Ships filled with manufactured goods—tools, weapons, and textiles—sailed from Europe to West Africa, where their cargo was traded for slaves. The slaves were shipped to the West Indies where they were sold. The profits bought sugar, coffee, cotton, and tobacco, which were sent back to Europe.

The merchants involved in shifting these goods and people from place to place made a profit on every transaction. The triangular trade became the main form of English overseas commerce. The English were becoming the most powerful businessmen in the world—and in the process, sugar was pouring into their homeland.

A confectioner's shop contained tempting treats such as jellies, sugar-plums, jams, and marmalades.

By the end of the seventeenth century, the English in the Caribbean were sending home almost fifty million pounds of sugar in addition to the sugar they were shipping directly to the North American colonies.

"Up until around 1680 sugar had remained pretty exclusive. It was for the elite, the rich, and the privileged," explains Sidney W. Mintz, Professor Emeritus of anthropology at The Johns Hopkins University. "But, from about 1700 onward you begin to see sugar percolating downward in the British social system to poor people, to ordinary people, to everyday people. And this is the same time that tea becomes important in British life."

Hot, sweet tea quickly became a popular drink throughout England. The British had two million acres of tea-producing plantations in India. They built roads and ports, brought in tools and equipment, and imported managers. Within a few decades, they had occupied large areas of the Indian subcontinent. Indian tea started as a business but ended up as the basis for ruling a colony.

During the 1700s, sugar developed a more everyday character and became the basis for English sweets. It included everything from candy to pastries and puddings. In 1760, Hannah Glasse, at that time England's equivalent to Julia Child, published a confectionery cookbook for the middle class. It is filled with recipes using sugar and clearly demonstrates that, by then, sugar was no longer considered a medicine or a spice limited to use in the kitchens of the rich.

No longer reserved for the elite, sugar cookies are a common treat for all classes.

When a Victorian family received an elegant guest, there was an array of sweets to accompany the afternoon tea.

JAM: FUELING THE ECONOMY?

Jam was extremely popular with the lowest economic groups in England; bread and jam fed working-class children for two out of three meals.

The English factory system promoted the use of jam for a number of reasons: it was ready to eat, so it did not take time away from work; it did not require heating, so no money was spent on fuel; and it provided a large number of calories at a very low price.

Anthropologist Sidney Mintz believes jam played an important role in the creation of a new economic structure in England. "As more women went out to work, there was a need to develop foods that would be available to the children who might be home without their parents, and speeding up food production at dinner became important," says Mintz. "One of those products was the factory production of jam. Because jam, unlike butter, doesn't go rancid, you can leave it on the table. A kid can get home and take some store-brought bread and smear it with jam. And this was important, again, in helping to develop a schedule, a time schedule, that suited the factory rather than the family, that suited the industrial workday, in the same way that tea was the first pause that refreshed. So jam on bread became the second pause that refreshed."

*Sweet and sticky, jam became an important self-serve meal
for children whose parents had entered the factories.*

The idea of a final sweet course came into fashion at the end of the 1600s but only among the richest level of European society. A dessert course, usually a pudding, only became part of the common meal during the late 1800s.

When the price of sugar dropped during the mid-1850s, sugar became the preservative of choice for the jam manufacturers. Suddenly their products could be mass-produced, and they became inexpensive enough to attract a large market.

The history of sugar in England has been repeated in many countries throughout the world, especially the English-speaking world. By the late 1880s, people in the United States were consuming sixty pounds of sugar per year. And whatever British capitalists learned about sugar as a source of profit, North American industrialists learned it faster. Whereas England had Barbados as a source for its sugar cane, the United States had Puerto Rico and Cuba in the Atlantic, and Hawaii and the Philippines in the Pacfic.

Many authorities believe that the sugar business that developed in the Caribbean was an important stage in the development of modern capitalism. It required the investment of large amounts of money, much of which was supplied by Dutch investors. The planters were often absentee businessmen who operated on borrowed money that usually came from big-city banks—and success was measured in profits. It established a system of world trade and helped put an end to the feudalism that for centuries had been the primary economic tradition in Europe.

As industrialists in the United States entered the sugar market, they turned to Puerto Rico, Cuba, Hawaii, and the Philippines as a source of sugar cane.

For centuries, no other commodity on the world market wielded as much political influence. Sugar affected almost every aspect of government policy from wages to wars in much the same way that oil does today.

"In many ways sugar is an ideal substance," said Mintz. "It serves to make a busy life seem less busy; in the pause that refreshes it seems to ease the change between work and rest; and it provides a quick sensation of fullness and satisfaction. No wonder the rich and powerful liked it so much and the poor learned to love it. It is symbolically powerful."

Today, more than one out of every ten calories consumed throughout the world is taken in the form of a sweet and that number is growing. It appears that the good life, and the rich life, is still the sweet life.

THE STORY OF
Wine
IN THE AMERICAS

In the year 1001, Leif Ericsson pushed his Viking longboat off the Greenland shore and sailed west. He landed on the northern coast of what we now call Newfoundland, Canada. Ericsson and his crew split up to do some exploring, and, at the end of the day, Tyrker the German reported that he had found wild grapes. Considering how far north Ericsson and his crew were, it is highly unlikely that Tyrker was looking at grapes. What he had probably found were cranberries. But Ericsson, like Columbus and most other explorers, discovered what he wanted to discover and accordingly named the place Vinland. Ericsson assumed that the continent would soon become a major wine-producing area. He wasn't wrong; just off a few hundred years on his estimated time of arrival.

All of the "classic" wine-grape varieties—from cabernet sauvignon to zinfandel—are part of a species that was domesticated about seven thousand years ago. The domestication took place somewhere in the mountains of what is now northwestern Iran.

Native Americans made fermented drinks from the agave plant and from corn, but they never developed a taste for fermented grape beverages. As a result, grapevines in America were left to evolve without human intervention. They were smaller than the fruits in Europe, did not taste the same, and sometimes grew in clusters like cherries, rather than in bunches. They were too sweet, too sour, or too bitter to make the wines that Europeans preferred.

Cabernet sauvignon grapes have become one of the best-known varieties of wine grape grown in the United States. The cabernet grape becomes a rich, darkly colored, berry flavored wine that is one of the most popular types of wine available.

For centuries wine had been the beverage of choice for the Spanish, and it was what Columbus's crew drank—he had dozens of casks on board. The wine he carried was fortified and similar to Madeira or sherry. It kept well during long sea voyages and had a solid kick. Wine was fundamental to Spanish culture, and more important, it was an essential part of Catholic ritual.

When the Spanish arrived in the Americas, they were surprised to find that the Native Americans, who lived in a land filled with wild grapevines, did not make wine. Some Spanish priests concluded that if God had not provided the natives with the ability to make wine, he must not have meant them to become Christians. Less theologically inclined settlers ignored the question and attempted to make wine from the grapes they found, but the results were dismal.

New Spain needed wine, and since the settlers could not depend on the local grapes, they brought in replacements from home. In 1524, at the settlement that would become Mexico City, Hernán Cortés, the commander of New Spain, imported vines from Europe, and ordered the Spanish settlers to plant one thousand grapevines for every hundred native laborers.

But Cortés's plan didn't work. The Mexican climate was too harsh and the Spanish settlers never came up with a significant harvest, at least not in the sixteenth or seventeenth centuries.

The Spanish government shelved its plans for the expansion of the Mexican vineyards and concentrated on South America. By the middle of the 1500s, a thriving wine industry existed in Peru, Chile, and Argentina. By the beginning of the seventeenth century, South American vineyards were big business and were exporting so much wine to Europe that the Spanish vintners back home felt threatened.

At the end of the 1500s, the English began building settlements in North America. Their new colonies were overrun with native grapevines, and it seemed possible that with a little work good wine would be as near as the next harvest.

Hernando Cortes, shown above, called the newly conquered lands in the Americas "New Spain" and set out to produce wine for the new colonists.

England and its American colonies got much of their wine from Spain and the Spanish vineyards in South America. If the English colonies in North America could produce wine, then England's dependence on Spanish imports could be broken. In terms of the wine business, North America might do for England what South America did for Spain. As early as 1609, the colonists at Jamestown were doing their best to make wine from the local grapes. But this was not an easy task.

Early attempts at wine making proved unsuccessful for American families in the colonies.

America's first vintners expected to make the dry and acidic-style wines of continental Europe, but the labrusca grape the English colonists were growing tasted more like grape jelly than European wine. When they used it to make wine the result was frightening. The settlers called the labrusca the "fox" grape, because of its heavy, musky scent.

Frustrated by the failure of Jamestown to produce drinkable wine, the British government passed a law requiring the settlers to "plant and maintain ten new vines each year until they have attained the art and experience of dressing a vineyard." In spite of the new law the English suspected that the colonists still did not know what they were doing and in 1620 sent the Virginians a group of French wine experts, along with a collection of European vine cuttings.

But even after the introduction of the European varieties and expert help, Virginia's vineyards continued to fail. In the humid summer weather the European vines succumbed to a variety of fungal diseases. In most years there was no grape harvest. After a few more attempts, including the distribution of winemaking manuals by the government, even the most enthusiastic colonial official gave up on the idea of a Virginia wine industry.

The experience was repeated up and down the Atlantic coast. Wine making in British North America, from the Carolinas to Massachusetts, had been tried and, by the end of the 1600s, abandoned. For refreshment, the colonists drank cider, rum, whiskey, and imported Madeira wine. A few intrepid farmers, mainly German and French immigrants who had some wine making experience, continued to cultivate the native vines, but without much success.

THOMAS JEFFERSON

In the years leading up to the American Revolution, the prospects for American wine remained bleak. But this did not dim the enthusiasm of prominent wine lovers like Benjamin Franklin and Thomas Jefferson. In the early years of the new republic, Jefferson established himself as a one-man committee for the improvement of American wine making.

Americans had become hard drinkers, and whiskey was the national beverage. Jefferson saw wine as the ideal "democratic drink," much preferable to distilled spirits, and throughout his life he remained confident that his home state of Virginia had a perfect climate for the cultivation of wine grapes. Jefferson repeatedly tried to produce wine on his estate and to encourage experiments by others. While Jefferson was a failure as a vintner, his encouragement helped to get the American wine industry going, even if the start was a bit shaky.

Since the 1740s, a few winemakers, most notably a Swiss immigrant named Jean Jacques Dufour, had been experimenting—and making small amounts of mediocre wine— with the Alexander grape, an accidental hybrid of European and American varieties.

By the beginning of the 1800s, agricultural knowledge had developed to the point where horticulturists, professional and amateur, had begun systematically breeding hybrid plants. Wine makers no longer had to depend on accidents in order to locate usable grape varieties. In 1823, John Adlum finally had some meaningful success with a hybrid called the Catawba, from which he produced and sold a reasonably drinkable wine. He sent the first bottle to Thomas Jefferson.

Thomas Jefferson, shown above in a portrait made of him during a trip to Paris, was one of America's earliest wine enthusiasts; he even attempted to produce wine on his Monticello estate in Virginia.

Wine tasters have the enviable job of testing the palatability of wine before the product is released to the market.

Nicholas Longworth, an Ohio lawyer and real estate millionaire turned vintner, made more than drinkable wine. He made American wine into a business, and in the process established the United States' reputation as a wine-growing nation. Longworth, who shared Thomas Jefferson's notion that wine could provide a healthy alternative to hard liquor, took the Catawba grape and made a sparkling wine from it. He then went on to establish the first commercially successful winery in the United States. By 1852, he was distributing his wines nationally and for a decade or so made Cincinnati the center of the American wine industry.

Meanwhile, in 1854, Ephraim Bull, an amateur botanist, introduced the Concord grape, which quickly became central to the wine-making industry in the Northeast. It became popular because of its resistance to disease rather than its taste—Concord is pure, foxy labrusca through and through.

In the South, wines made from the Scuppernong grape became quite popular.

California's Napa Valley has a Mediterranean climate that proved to be a perfect growing environment for the grapevines that produce high-quality wines.

Among them was a wine known as Virginia Dare which was named after the first English child born in the Americas. A native wine industry—and, oddly enough, one based largely on American grapes—had developed.

But the reign of East Coast, Southern, and Midwestern wines, based on American grapes or hybrids, was short lived. California was gaining fast, and by the 1870s, Cincinnati's brief dominance as the center of the American wine industry was over.

While the early history of wine making on the East Coast is the story of people trying to make top-quality wine in a difficult environment, the story on the West Coast—especially in California—is very different. California's northern valleys are perfectly suited to the cultivation of the European grape varieties; in fact, they might be the best-suited locations in the world.

In northern Mexico and the Baja, Spanish missionaries were cultivating European vines—without major

The Concord grape is a hearty variety chosen by wine makers more often for its resistance to disease than for its taste, which is heavier and muskier than more delicate varieties.

problems. In 1769, the Franciscans moved north and found California hospitable. Within a decade, missions as far north as the San Francisco Bay were producing wine, though not in commercial quantities. California's Mediterranean climate was generally free of the fungal diseases that plagued grapevines in the east. The mission vineyards were small but successful.

By the time the Mexican government secularized the southern California missions in 1830, a small wine industry had begun to develop. Jean-Louis Vignes, a French immigrant, found the local mission grape limiting, and began to import "classic" varieties from Europe, which he grew successfully. The Los Angeles-based firm of Kohler and Frohling, following Vignes's lead, planted European varieties and aggressively marketed their products back east. California began to develop a reputation as a wine-producing area.

In 1848, the United States took California from Mexico, and adventurers poured into the new territory. When gold was discovered in 1849 the majority of people arriving were prospectors; a few got rich and moved on but by the end of the rush most of the prospectors were looking for a new way to earn a living.

Agoston Haraszthy, a Hungarian immigrant who had been a county sheriff, gold assayer, and state representative, believed that northern California was ideal for growing wine grapes and began importing hundreds of European vines. The Buena Vista vineyard he founded in 1857 is still operating.

San Francisco's waterfront, in the late 1800s.

During the 1870s, the California wine industry centered itself around San Francisco Bay, making it the leading wine-producing area in the United States. Larger firms were buying up smaller vineyards, and the state's first large-scale industrial wineries were being established. Many were staffed by Chinese laborers who had been building the railroads. California was developing a worldwide reputation, and exports were beginning to grow.

Following pages: Green, red, and purple vines decorate the vineyard in the bright colors of autumn.

PROHIBITION YEARS

From our earliest colonial days, the idea of temperance had been part of American culture, but it was a minority view. An 1823 survey concluded that Americans were hard drinkers—consuming seven-and-one-half gallons of distilled spirits per person annually, which is about three times greater than what we presently consume. During the second half of the 1800s, however, anti-alcohol sentiment became widespread, but even Americans suspicious of hard liquor thought of wine as less of a threat.

The temperance movement of the late nineteenth and early twentieth centuries was less selective; it condemned wine as just another flavor of "Demon Rum." When the Eighteenth Amendment, prohibiting the production and sale of alcoholic beverages in America, was finally ratified, wine makers were not spared.

Prohibition began in 1920 and ended the careers of many wine makers. But a loophole in the Volstead Act allowed for the home production of two hundred gallons of wine a year, and some California grape growers found a way to cater to their new consumers. Instead of selling bulk wine, they sold grape concentrate, or compressed-grape bricks, which were conveniently packaged along with a yeast capsule and explicit instructions telling the customer exactly how to avoid making wine. These kits were a huge success.

Other winemakers were able to ride out the dry years as producers of sacramental or "medicinal" wines. One of the wineries that shifted into the making of sacramental wine was Beaulieu Vineyards of Rutherford in Napa Valley, founded during the early 1900s by Georges de Latour, a chemist from a French grape-growing family. During Prohibition, Beaulieu prospered; de Latour was under contract to supply altar wine to the Archdiocese of San Francisco.

Churches across the country looked to the Archdiocese of San Francisco for their own altar wine and San Francisco referred those requests to Beaulieu. De Latour was devoted to making the best wine possible and he saw no reason to lower his standards because it was being sold for use in church ritual. Accordingly, he shipped hundreds of boxcars of his finest wine to churches in the Midwest and along the East Coast. As those boxcars passed through Chicago many of them mysteriously disappeared. Somehow, the fine vintages that were being presented during the morning mass in church were also showing up during the evening meal in the speakeasies.

When Prohibition ended in 1933, de Latour was producing wines of excellent quality and his socially connected wife began promoting them to San Francisco society. But de Latour was always interested in improving his wine. In 1938, he hired André Tchelistcheff, a Russian-born, French-trained wine expert who had studied at the Pasteur Institute in Paris. Tchelistcheff revolutionized wine making throughout California and is considered to be the father of the industry.

Fine wine was made during Prohibition but, in theory, only for sacramental use.

The unpopular Eighteenth Amendment to the Constitution made the possession or sale of alcohol illegal.

After the repeal of Prohibition in 1933, the U.S. wine industry was in sad shape. With few exceptions, the wine-making concerns that had survived were left with little interest in producing quality wines, and once freed of legal restrictions, they were primarily interested in making their wines a competitive consumer product.

And American tastes had changed. The generation that grew up during Prohibition thought of wine as something cheap, sweet, and alcoholic. And the wine industry, struggling to get back on its feet was not about to try changing the consumer's mind. A few of the older Napa Valley wineries went back to making dry wines in the French style, but for the most part, California's wine producers were out to give the people what they wanted, or what the winemakers thought they wanted.

In the 1960s, Italian Swiss Colony, whose winery gift shop is shown here, was one of the most prolific California producers

After World War II, wine making became big business. During the 1940s and 1950s corporate consolidation of the United States wine industry got underway, with large firms buying up small wineries and vineyards. At the same time, giant wine-making concerns, like Ernest & Julio Gallo and Italian Swiss Colony, were battling for market share.

All of these companies were making similar products—either sweet, fortified wines that competed with cocktails or simple table wines. They were struggling to find the fastest, cleanest, most efficient ways of growing, harvesting, making, and marketing their product.

The search for efficiency sparked a renaissance in wine-making technology. The California firms, with an insatiable need for qualified staff to run their wine-making operations, funded the Department of Viticulture and Enology at the University of California at Davis. That department, in turn, became a center of innovation for wine-making technology, doing basic research on the climate of California and developing high-yield grape varieties, and new fermentation and aging techniques. Davis provided the large wine makers with the technology and personnel they needed.

Wine making has become an enormous industry thanks in part to the efforts of California wineries, who produced this ad on pairing food with wine.

AN UNINTENDED EXPORT

During the 1840s, a North American fungal disease in the form of a powdery mildew began to afflict European vineyards. It reduced the grape yields and, during the 1850s, almost destroyed the chardonnay and cabernet sauvignon harvests. French farmers learned to control the fungus with applications of sulfur, and by 1860 the industry had gotten back on its feet.

But it was only a brief remission. During the 1860s, a far more serious problem appeared. Grapevines across Europe began to wither and slowly die, and by the 1880s many of France's vineyards were in desperate condition. French researchers found the source of the disease—a voracious, fast-breeding aphid, native to North America. It had probably been brought to Europe in shipments of experimental vine cuttings. The aphid, named *phylloxera*, "the devastator," fed on the roots of the vines, slowly killing them—the French wine industry was on the brink of total destruction.

Scientists in France discovered that most of the grape species native to the Americas had

In the 1840s, a fungal disease spread throughout vineyards of Europe, destroying the grapes and devastating the wine industry.

evolved alongside *phylloxera* and had developed at least some resistance to it. At about the same time, Texas horticulturist T. V. Munson found that European vines could be grafted to American roots, and would still bear fruit. French winegrowers put his work into practice, and began to import tens of thousands of American vines for use as rootstock. But many of the vines imported from America to save the French vines carried *phylloxera*.

In the end, the French wine industry was saved. But in the process the French growers spread the aphid throughout Europe, forcing the entire continent and eventually the entire world—including California—to graft their *vinifera* vines to the aphid-resistant American roots.

Chile and some parts of Washington State, for reasons not well understood, were spared infestation by the aphids. In every other wine-growing area in the world the vines are grafted onto American rootstocks, bred especially for their resistance to *phylloxera*.

By the beginning of the 1960s, it was clear that American tastes were changing again. Whether the cause was Kennedy-era sophistication, a growing middle class, or general changes in American cuisine, is unknown, but what is clear is that consumers began developing an interest in classic European-style wines. Since Prohibition ended, the market had been driven by sales of fortified wines like Ripple and Thunderbird. In 1967, table wines pulled ahead.

During the late 1960s and early 1970s hundreds of small boutique wineries were founded in California's Napa Valley and neighboring Sonoma County. In the process, California became synonymous with premium American wine making.

Young wine makers, many of whom had been educated at Davis and had started their careers at the larger California wineries, became interested in growing premium grapes. They were joined by an increasing number of wealthy hobbyists, who had turned to serious wine making as second careers.

These boutiques explored various European styles, and defined Napa Valley as the home of artisanal wine making in the United States. By the mid-1970s, many of them believed their wines could compete with the best European wines. And soon they were able to prove it.

In 1976, Steven Spurrier, an Englishman who ran an influential wineshop in Paris, organized a blind tasting of California wines. The judges were a group of leading French critics. Until the day of the tasting, Spurrier neglected to tell them that for comparison he had included a number of the finest French wines. To everyone's surprise, when the labels were revealed, a 1973 Cabernet from Stag's Leap Wine Cellars in California took the prize, beating out the best of the French.

Time magazine called the tasting "The

Judgment of Paris." It proved that American wines could compete successfully against the best wines of France; but more important, it illustrated the fact that in just a few decades American wines had progressed to a point where the California wine industry was raising the worldwide standard for wine making.

There was an explosion of interest in California wines in general, and a special fascination with those produced in Napa Valley. Beginning in the late 1970s, some of the top European wine makers began developing joint ventures with their American counterparts or building their own wineries in California.

The new generation of Napa Valley wine makers had been a wealthy one to begin with, but during the late 1970s and 1980s even more money poured into the area. Celebrities bought vineyards and wineries, and larger concerns hired star architects to design major new winery buildings.

Pinot noir (top) and Riesling grapes are a couple of star varieties in the world of wine making.

While the new wave of winemaking did not immediately transform the United States into a wine-drinking nation, it did make wine drinking fashionable, and wine became more and more popular through the 1980s and 1990s.

Today, wine is being made in every state except Alaska and Wyoming, and winemakers across the United States have turned their talents toward the production of premium wines. Following the history of major wine-growing areas in Europe, regions in the United States have begun to focus on specific grapes: New York State, for example, has become prime Riesling territory, while Oregon has focused on pinot noir. And Virginia, the state that proved so frustrating for America's first wine makers, has become a thriving center of wine production. These days, there are even wineries at Thomas Jefferson's Monticello. Jefferson would be proud—American winemakers have managed to make some of his dreams come true.

PHOTO CREDITS